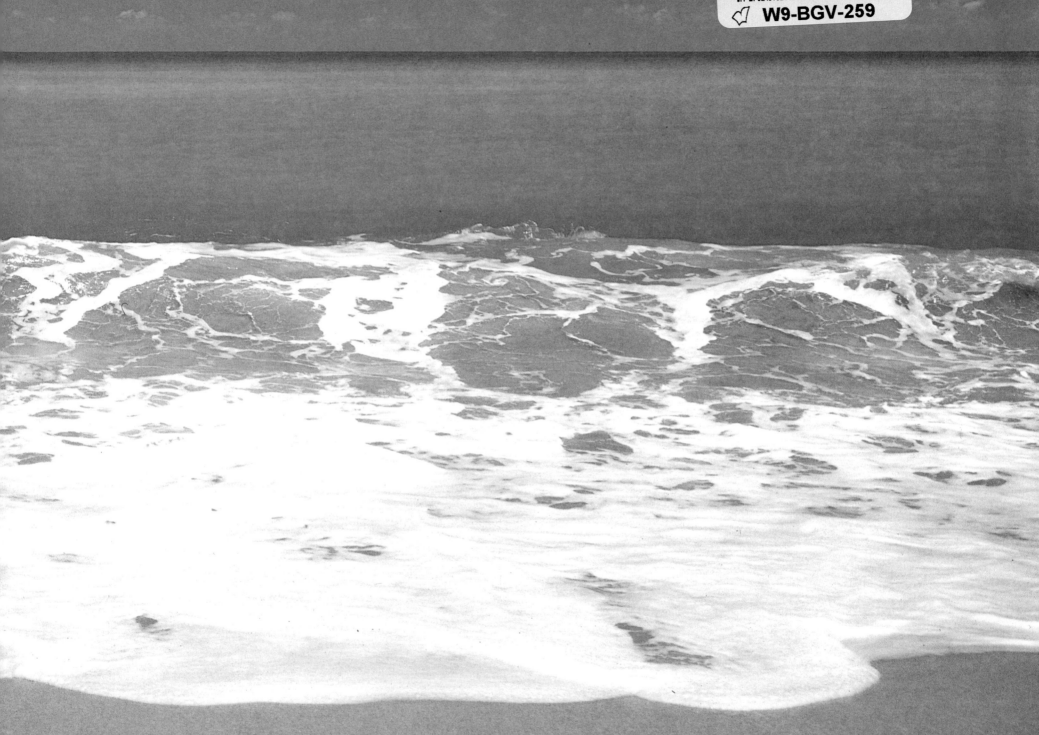

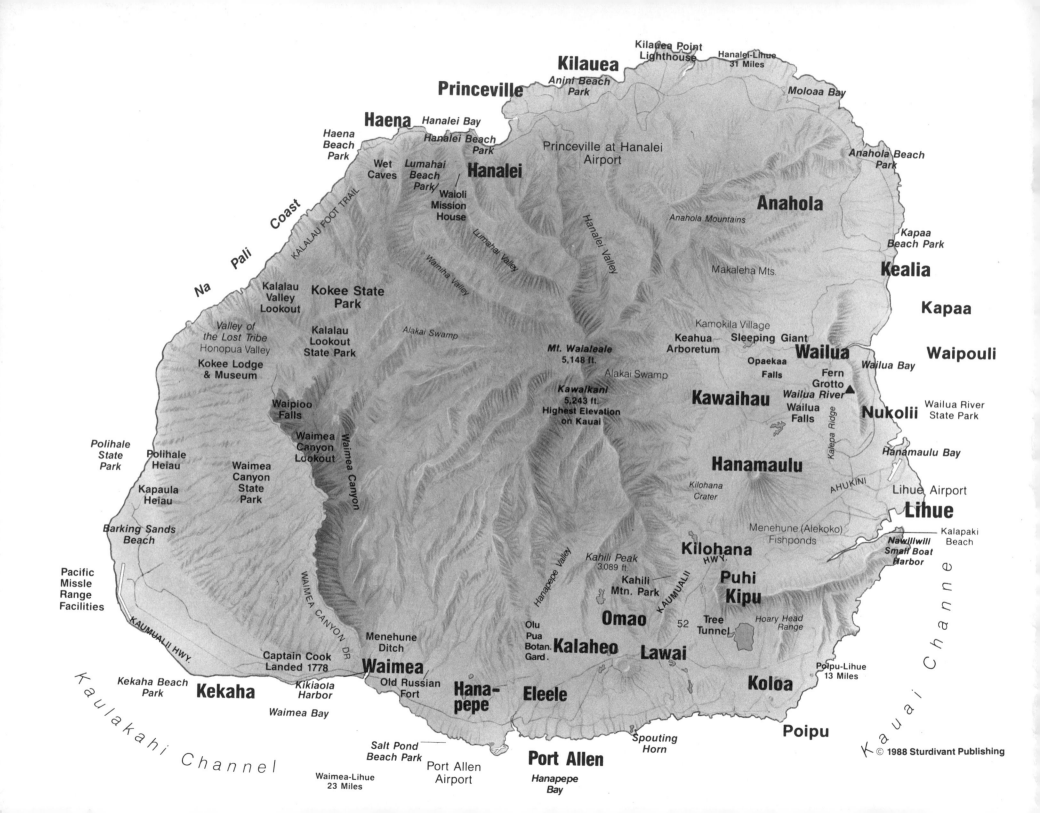

Kilauea Point Lighthouse
Hanalei-Lihue 31 Miles

Kilauea

Anini Beach Park

Princeville

Moloaa Bay

Haena
Hanalei Bay

Haena Beach Park

Hanalei Beach Park

Hanalei
Princeville at Hanalei Airport

Anahola Beach Park

Wet Caves
Lumahai Beach Park
Waioli Mission House

Na Pali Coast
KALALAU FOOT TRAIL

Lumahai Valley

Hanalei Valley

Anahola

Anahola Mountains

Na Pali

Wainiha Valley

Kapaa Beach Park

Makaleha Mts.

Kealia

Kalalau Valley Lookout
Kokee State Park

Alakai Swamp

Kamokila Village
Keahua Arboretum
Sleeping Giant

Kapaa

Valley of the Lost Tribe
Honopua Valley

Kalalau Lookout State Park

Mt. Waialeale 5,148 ft.

Alakai Swamp

Opaekaa Falls

Wailua

Waipouli

Kokee Lodge & Museum

Kawaikani 5,243 ft. Highest Elevation on Kauai

Kawaihau

Fern Grotto
Wailua River
Wailua Falls

Wailua Bay

Waipioo Falls

Waimea Canyon Lookout

Waimea Canyon

Nukolii

Wailua River State Park

Polihale State Park
Polihale Heiau

Kalepa Ridge

Hanamaulu Bay

Kapaula Heiau

Waimea Canyon State Park

Hanamaulu

Kilohana Crater

AHUKINI

Lihue Airport

Barking Sands Beach

Menehune (Alekoko) Fishponds

Lihue

Pacific Missle Range Facilities

WAIMEA CANYON DR.

Kahili Peak 3,089 ft.

Kilohana
HWY.

Kalapaki Beach

Nawiliwili Small Boat Harbor

Hanapepe Valley

Kahili Mtn. Park

Puhi
Kipu

KAUMUALII

52
Tree Tunnel

Hoary Head Range

KAUMUALII HWY.

Captain Cook Landed 1778

Menehune Ditch

Olu Pua Botan. Gard.

Omao

Lawai

Poipu-Lihue 13 Miles

Kekaha Beach Park

Waimea
Old Russian Fort

Kalaheo

Koloa

Kekaha
Kikiaola Harbor

Hana-pepe

Eleele

Waimea Bay

Kaulakahi Channel

Salt Pond Beach Park

Port Allen

Spouting Horn

Poipu

Port Allen Airport

Waimea-Lihue 23 Miles

Hanapepe Bay

Kauai Channel

© 1988 Sturdivant Publishing

SAND AND SEA (end sheets): The beach at
Polihale State Park, on the western end of Kauai, seems
to go on forever. It is one of the finest beaches in the state.
BEACH TRACKS (above): A line of footprints
fades into the sand at this isolated beach located
between Princeville and Hanalei.

2

KAUA'I

A Many Splendored Island

Photographed by Douglas Peebles
Written by Ronn Ronck

Art Direction by Bill Fong
Designed by Leo Gonzalez and
Peter Matsukawa

Mutual Publishing of Honolulu

BEFORE THE DANCE (opposite page): These young women are members of a hula school in Lihue and are waiting to perform in the annual June 11 Kamehameha Day Parade.

Foreword

Stephen Gnazzo

Welcome to *Kauai: A Many Splendored Island*, a book that captures the real Kauai: our natural beauty, historical places, and special mix of people and cultures.

We have a history of being unique and independent. King Kamehameha I, for instance, failed to conquer Kauai—the only island in the Hawaiian archipelago to escape his army.

The theme of uniqueness and independence continues today in the pride and commitment of Kauai's people to continue the traditions, to preserve our spectacular beauty, and to retain the rural character of the island.

We are regarded by residents and many visitors as the most natural, green and unspoiled of all the Hawaiian islands.

I believe that if we are diligent in identifying and preserving our unique assets, we will guarantee for the future, both our economic prosperity and very fine quality of life. By expanding our concept of tourism to include a new emphasis on cultural tourism, this goal can be achieved.

Therefore, I invite you to enjoy *Kauai: A Many Splendored Island* and to experience our way of life through the beautiful pages of this book. It is the presentation of all that is unique to us.

Aloha nui loa,

JoAnn A. Yukimura
Mayor, County of Kauai

Fourth Edition—June 1989
LCC 85062694
Mutual Publishing Company of Honolulu
2055 N. King Street
Honolulu, Hawaii 96819

Contents

HANALEI VALLEY. From the lookout above
Hanalei Valley there is a panoramic view across green taro
fields to the distant mountains. Today the taro farmers
on Kauai's north shore grow about seventy percent of the
state's entire supply.

Introduction

The island of Kauai is a sequestered place, located at the northwest end of the Hawaiian chain, separated from the islands to the southeast by the tempestuous Kauai Channel. An integral part of the Hawaiian Islands, Kauai remained independent from the rule of chiefs on the southeastern islands for generations. Only in 1810 did it formally become a part of the united Hawaiian Kingdom. After that the Garden Island was slowly drawn closer to the other islands by the promise of a better economic future and because steamships at last could challenge the Kauai Channel more successfully than had sailing ships.

There is a sense of history about Kauai, visible in the ancient ruins in sacred lower Wailua Valley, the remains of the sugar mill at Koloa, the crumbled walls of the long-abandoned Russian fort at Waimea, and the guardian lighthouse at Kilauea Point.

The physical evidence of history is discovered amidst stunning natural beauty, in settings which cannot be duplicated anywhere else. The gentle sandy curve of Hanalei Bay, given privacy by a backup of perpendicular cliffs, has been praised in song since the earliest of times. There is the memorable celestial evening sunlight slanting across the ranch lands of Kipu. There is the wild collision of Pacific swells against Na Pali. There is the multicolored Waimea Valley, cutting ever deeper into the heart of Kauai, culminating in the spectacular Waimea Canyon.

Kauai remains a memorable secluded Hawaiian place, even in today's world of convenient transportation. To see it is to begin to understand the ancient mele or poem which begins, "Beautiful is Kauai beyond compare."

In the following pages, through the words of Ronn Ronck and the photographs of Douglas Peebles, the history and beauty of the Garden Island can be found. Kauai has never been captured any better.

Edward Joesting

Edward Joesting is the author of *Kauai: The Separate Kingdom* and *Hawaii: An Uncommon History.* He also collaborated with the photographer Ansel Adams on two books about Hawaii.

NEIGHBORHOOD CAFE (opposite page): A bicycle is parked in front of Sharon's Saimin Bowl in Kapaa. This family-run restaurant has long been popular with both residents and visitors.

A Promise Kept

Beautiful Kauai. It is an island for the senses, a tropical paradise blessed with sunny weather, majestic mountains, and wide sandy beaches. The oldest major landfall in the Hawaiian chain, Kauai's great volcano erupted under the Pacific millions of years ago and spread out into a rough circular shape.

Eventually the lava cooled and, when the flames darkened, the winds and rains took over. Heavy downpours carved canyons thousands of feet deep and sent streams and wild rivers rushing to the sea. The island then turned green with vegetation and the birds came, nesting in the thick protected forests.

By the time the first human settlers arrived, Kauai was indeed a garden. Because theirs was a seagoing culture, most of the people decided to live by the shoreline. Others followed the rivers into the interior and built their houses in the mountain valleys.

Thousands of years went by, then outsiders came in tall sailing ships. They brought iron, horses, cattle, and a new religion. Sugarcane and pineapple were planted, grown, and harvested. The forests became farms and the villages turned into towns.

Such changes, however, have been slow and there are seacoasts and landscapes on Kauai which still resemble those that were seen by the earliest Hawaiians. Today's visitors can also discover the charming rural atmosphere of Kauai that is enhanced by the down-to-earth warmth and hospitality of those who live and work there.

Former mayor Tony Kunimura popularized a slogan for the Garden Island. It is *Kauai—A Promise Kept*.

"Kauai," he explains, "is the only island in the Hawaiian chain that has fulfilled the promise of its history and traditions. This is where visitors can find the true spirit of yesterday's Polynesia without sacrificing the comforts which are available in modern high-quality destination resorts."

During the past several years, Douglas Peebles and I have driven and walked over much of Kauai. We have hiked over long-forgotten trails, camped beside remote cascading waterfalls, and flown across the misty mountaintops by plane and helicopter. At other times we have explored more civilized territory, visiting towns and plantations and meeting the local people who make this special place their home.

On the following pages you will find a portrait of the Kauai we found during our travels, presented in words and photographs. We invite you to experience the Garden Island with us. Beautiful Kauai. It is a paradise waiting to be shared, a promise kept.

Ronn Ronck

WATER LILIES (opposite page): These water lilies bloom in the Kiahuna Plantation Gardens in Poipu.

COUNTRY HOMESTEAD: *This ranch house outside of Kapaa is typical of those found in the rural areas of Kauai.*

14

Volcanic Origins

Pele, the temperamental fire goddess, stands at the center of Hawaiian mythology. She was born as a flame from the union of the earth mother, Haumea, and the sky father, Wakea. The most beautiful of the goddesses, Pele is often associated with the volcanic origins of the islands.

The Hawaiian archipelago is a chain of over a hundred islands, reefs, and shoals stretching 1,523 miles southeast to northwest. The eight main islands, in order of size, are Hawaii (which gives the chain its name), Maui, Oahu, Kauai, Molokai, Lanai, Niihau, and Kahoolawe.

One of Pele's earliest homes was Kauai, which is formed from a single shield volcano that has become deeply eroded with time and further volcanic action. The goddess later traveled to Oahu, Maui, and Hawaii (often called the Big Island), leaving behind a trail of volcanoes that flickered out and died. Only Kilauea and Mauna Loa on the Big Island remain active today.

When Kauai first broke through the surface of the Pacific, it was but barren rock. The top of the volcano was a crater that measured over twenty miles across. Erupting lava gradually filled the crater to its brim and spilled over to the south, flowing to the sea. A smaller crater burst on the southeastern flank and was eventually covered with another blanket of lava.

Over incredible lengths of time, living seeds fell upon the land and took root. Trade winds brought some of these seeds; others drifted upon the sea or were carried by birds. Most of these plants thrived in Kauai's mild tropical climate, its rich volcanic soil, and regular rainfall. Today, because of Hawaii's isolation from the continents, more than twenty-five hundred kinds of plants exist that are found nowhere else on earth.

Kauai's isolation also helped the evolution of unique land birds. Ten families of birds are represented in the islands and one family, the Hawaiian honeycreepers, are found nowhere else in the world. Of the land mammals, only the bat and the monk seal were here before the first Polynesian settlers.

Mt. Waialeale, once the eruptive center of the island, shows only faint evidence of the fires that used to burn far below. There are patterns of black ash on some of the vertical cliffs, and molten rocks lie twisted deep within the interior.

Kauai's highest peak, Kawaikini on Mt. Waialeale, is 5,243 feet above sea level. This is probably close to the original height of the mountain when the volcanic eruptions finally ceased.

Kawaikini's summit plateau is called the Alakai Swamp. It extends for ten miles northwestward from the volcanic birthplace of the island and ends about three miles from the sea. Much of the plateau is defined by sharp cliff walls and the heads of major valleys.

Mt. Waialeale is often called the wettest spot on earth. Deep in the jungle, far from the sunny beaches that characterize the rest of the island, the summit averages over 450 inches of rainfall each year. Clouds usually ring Mt. Waialeale, a name that's translated as "rippling waters." Once a pit of intense fire, Pele's former home is now a place of abundant rain. From this great mountainous source the Garden Island maintains its healthy bloom. ■

*MOUNTAIN CLOUD COVER (opposite page):
In the center of Kauai, the mountains are often surrounded
by clouds. FOREST FERNS (above): The interior forests
are home for a variety of ferns which thrive in
the abundant rainfall.*

16

MOUNT WAIALEALE (above): Mt. Waialeale, officially
the wettest area in the world, averages 451 inches of rainfall
annually. WAIALEALE WATERFALL (right): This high
waterfall is among hundreds caused by the heavy runoff
from Mt. Waialeale. MOUNTAIN TOP (opposite page):
The summit of Mt. Waialeale.

HANALEI WATERFALL (left): This waterfall drops into Hanalei Valley and helps to irrigate its taro fields.
WILDERNESS WATERFALL (above): Mt. Waialeale is the ultimate source of countless waterfalls on Kauai.

KAPAA STREAM (right): Loose rocks line the bed of this meandering stream above Kapaa.

CENTRAL CASCADE (left): This waterfall is
located in the central mountain portion of Kauai.
SCENIC VALLEY (above): From any direction Hanalei
Valley is one of the most scenic areas of the island.
MOUNTAIN CLOUDS (opposite page): A river of clouds
flows down the side of Mt. Waialeale.

Hawaiian Ancestors

uring ancient times the Hawaiians cleared a trail that led to the top of Mt. Waialeale. They traveled by canoe to the end of the Wailua River and then climbed the ridges by foot. It was an exhausting and often hazardous trip.

At the summit was a temple, or heiau, dedicated to Kane, the creation god identified with sunlight, fresh water, and the living forest. Offerings were placed on its altar, a large slab of rock that is still in place today. Nearby is a shallow pond that flows downward into the stream that cuts deeply through Wainiha Valley.

The heiau on Mt. Waialeale was built by the earliest inhabitants of Kauai. They arrived from the Marquesas Islands in their double-hulled canoes beginning about A.D. 500. By about A.D. 750 all of the Hawaiian Islands had been settled. Later, a second migration of people from Tahiti came between A.D. 1000 and A.D. 1250. Chants tell of regular ocean voyages between Tahiti and Hawaii during this latter period.

Legends say the first landing place was at the mouth of the Wailua River. This fertile region became sacred to the island's high chiefs and they constructed the heiau on Mt. Waialeale to thank the gods for their good fortune. Other villages were located along the river.

It is certain that the early Hawaiians also made visits to the beautiful natural amphitheatre that is today known as the Fern Grotto. Modern-day visitors to Kauai now take motorized boat trips three miles up the Wailua River to see the Fern Grotto for themselves.

Kauai's pioneer settlers were well provided for in their new home. There were flat stretches of land on which to build their villages and

wide beaches to pull up their canoes. The forests provided wood, fruits, and small wildlife for hunting. The ocean and reef areas sheltered a wide variety of seafood.

Fishing was an important means of obtaining food for the ancient people of Kauai. The men often sailed far from shore in their canoes while the women and children remained within the inner reef to gather shellfish, sea urchins, and octopus. Fishponds were kept well stocked.

Ancient Kauai society was divided into classes. People were born to their class and seldom changed status in life. Chiefs, determined by the geneology of both parents, governed with a strict hand and punishment for breaking a law was usually severe. Professional warriors were also usually of the highest, or alii, class. On a descending scale were the kahunas, or skilled craftsmen, and then the commoners who made up the major share of the population.

There was no written language. History and traditions were passed orally from generation to generation, reserved in chants, stories, and the dances of the hula. It is through these arts that we know what life was like on Kauai before the Europeans arrived in the eighteenth century. ■

KAMOKILA VILLAGE (opposite page): On the banks of the Wailua River sits Kamokila Village. It is a modern recreation of an ancient Hawaiian settlement. CONCH BLOWER (above): The blowing of a conch shell is the traditional way to begin a hula performance.

HANAPEPE FARMER (opposite page): A farmer
stands in front of his Hanapepe Valley taro farm.
COLLECTING SALT (above): At Salt Pond Beach Park,
near Hanapepe, salt is gathered using the same methods
as the early Hawaiians.

HULA HANDS (above): A dancer tells a story with her
hands during a hula performance at Kee Beach. DRUM
BEATS (opposite page): Chanting and the sound of a pahu,
or drum, provides a rhythm for the dancer.

Captain James Cook visited Kauai on his third Pacific voyage. His ships, the Resolution and the Discovery, had left Tahiti on December 7, 1777, and anchored at a small, treeless, and uninhabited island on December 25. Cook stayed there through the end of the year and named it Christmas Island before sailing north.

On January 18, 1778, just after daybreak, the island of Oahu was sighted. The ships tried to find a hospitable cove but the winds were too light for the sails. The same day Kauai and Niihau were seen to the northwest.

Upon sailing closer to Kauai the next morning, it was learned that the islands were inhabited. Native islanders, in canoes, went alongside the ships. They refused to go aboard but offered up fish, pigs, and yams. In return the Englishmen threw down nails and other metal items.

Cook ordered his ships to sail along the southern coast of Kauai until they found a safe anchorage. The canoes followed and hundreds more of the islanders were seen lining the shores. When the ships finally came to anchor on January 20, off what is today Waimea, a few of the islanders had become brave enough to go aboard.

Cook went ashore on January 21 and the islanders greeted him warmly. His visit corresponded with a celebration of the god Lono, whose arrival on a floating island had been foretold. Some islanders prostrated themselves on the ground until he told them to rise. They treated Cook with the respect reserved for their highest chiefs. Later there was an exchange of gifts.

Early the next morning Cook walked inland with his ship's surgeon, William Anderson, and the expedition's young artist, John Webber. About a half-mile from shore the party was shown a Hawaiian temple or heiau. On the stone platform was a long grass hut containing wooden images and a tall wood-framed oracle tower hung with strips of bark cloth. They returned to the beach by another route, continuing to explore the inviting countryside.

Waimea itself was a fairly large village. There were about sixty grass houses near the shore and another forty spread out in back of the main settlement. It was a tidy, well-organized community.

News of the foreigners travelled fast on Kauai and soon Waimea was full of traders from more remote villages. Cook wrote in his journal that a single nail was able to buy two small pigs. Soon the Resolution and Discovery had taken on needed provisions.

High winds and rain began threatening Cook's anchorage on January 22 and the next morning the ships were taken out beyond the choppy surf. The rough weather made it difficult to return to Waimea, and the two ships spent the next six days tacking back and forth in the channel between Kauai and Niihau.

Eventually Captain Cook gave up on getting back to Kauai and he found a safe anchorage at Niihau where he could obtain more fresh water. Here, too, the natives were friendly and just as interested in trading meat, fruit, and yams for iron. The population was estimated to be about five hundred, quite small in comparison to the thirty thousand estimated to live on Kauai.

The officers had planned to stay longer on Niihau but that evening the anchor of the Resolution broke free and the ship drifted away from the island in the night. Not wanting to spend several more days trying to make it back to shore, Cook ordered both ships to set sail. Starting around noon, the expedition set off toward the north and disappeared behind the horizon.

Eight months later Captain Cook returned to the Sandwich Islands, which he had named after his patron, the Earl of Sandwich, First Lord of the British Admiralty. He spent his last days on the Big Island and was killed there during a skirmish at Kealakekua Bay between his men and a group of Hawaiians on February 14, 1779. ■

MISSION HOUSE (opposite page): The Waioli Mission House, completed in 1837, was the first American-style house built in Hanalei. It is now open to the public as a museum.

30

Canyons and Valleys

aptain Cook never saw Waimea Canyon. Although his two ships anchored only a few miles away in 1778, he and his crew had little time for island sightseeing. Replenishing the ships with food and fresh water was a more important task.

Explorations of the interior countryside were left to later travelers who traced the Waimea River, the longest in Hawaii, up into the mountains. They returned with glowing reports of a deep gorge nearly twenty-five hundred feet deep and ten miles wide. Waterfalls plummeted over the high cliffs and the erosion of the ages had painted the walls a range of soft earth colors.

As the years went by, descriptions of Waimea Canyon spread throughout the world. It became an attraction for the hardiest of visitors, many of whom thought it looked like a miniature version of the Grand Canyon. The comparison spawned its own legend and today Waimea Canyon is often called "The Grand Canyon of the Pacific."

From the Waimea Canyon Lookout visitors can get a clear view in both directions and to the stream that meanders far below. The head of the canyon is upstream from the lookout, and the lava flows directly across on the western side are cut by countless dikes.

Farther up the winding road, to an altitude of four thousand feet, is the Kalalau Valley Lookout. Viewers can look down the valley toward the ocean. The heads of Waimea Canyon and Kalalau Valley are slowly eroding toward each other and millions of years from now they will be joined.

Kalalau is the longest and broadest valley — about two miles across — along Kauai's northern Na Pali Coast. Until the 1920s an isolated group of Hawaiians lived in this valley, and stonework and still-terraced taro pond sites recall their presence.

The area is now part of Na Pali State Park and a limited number of campers are allowed into Kalalau Valley at a time. Some start from Haena on the Hanalei side of the island and hike along Na Pali Coast. Others arrive at the

valley's entrance by motorized rubber raft. Tents can be pitched in the forests, near old rock platforms and walls, or on the beach.

Kokee State Park, a 4,345-acre wilderness preserve that borders Waimea Canyon State Park's eighteen hundred acres, was officially established in 1952. It offers visitors a cool, crisp sanctuary at the four-thousand-foot level. Around the turn of the century sandalwood loggers and ranchers stripped the landscape until the loss of wooded lands began to effect the natural watershed.

Foresters later replanted the Kokee trees but newly introduced species choked out much of the surviving native plants. The forest lands at Kokee are now much different than they were before the loggers came, but lease residents and park visitors have made the park one of the most popular recreational areas on the island.

Although most park visitors are daytime sightseers there are an estimated forty-five miles of cleared trails for those with a desire to remain a little longer to explore the forests. Some of the trails are easy walks to lookout points while others seem to meander forever through the surrounding woodlands. One trail crosses the thickets and bogs of Alakai Swamp to a spot where hikers can see all the way to Hanalei. ∎

KALALAU VALLEY (opposite page): Kalalau Valley, seen here from the lookout at Kokee, is the largest valley on Kauai's scenic Na Pali Coast. PASSION FLOWER (above): A common passion flower blooms in Waimea Canyon.

WAIMEA CANYON: *Waimea Canyon is ten miles long, about a mile wide, and 3600 feet deep. It originally began as a crack on the flank of Kauai's great volcano. The earth tones of its cliffs are due to vegetation and soil that has eroded over millions of years.*

CANYON FOREST (above): The ravines of Waimea
Canyon are overgrown with kukui nut trees which follow
stream beds down the cliffs.

RIVER BED (left): A dried stream bed has left its
imprint on the canyon floor. OLOKELE CANYON
(above): Olokele Canyon, which meets the Waimea River
as it flows out of Waimea Canyon, drains a portion of the
Alakai Swamp.

35

36

GRAND SCENERY (above): Waimea Canyon reveals
spectacular scenes from any angle. HANAKOA STREAM
(right): Hanakoa Stream is a good resting place for hikers
traveling Na Pali Coast trail. TOWARD WAIMEA
(opposite page): A dramatic view from the canyon toward
the town of Waimea.

38

The Russians Are Coming

Close to the mouth of the Waimea River, on the east bank, sit the ruins of an old lava-rock fort. This was once Fort Elizabeth, built in 1816 by an ambitious German who wanted Russia to annex the island. Although not a very impressive site today, it recalls a fascinating chapter in the early history of Kauai.

At the turn of the nineteenth century the Russian American Company, an agency of Imperial Russia, was granted a monopoly to undertake fur trading in North America. The firm set up its headquarters at Sitka, Alaska, and its supply ships sailed regularly across the Pacific.

On January 31, 1815, one of these Russian ships, the Bering, was caught in a storm off Waimea and crashed into the beach. It could not be refloated and its cargo was confiscated by Kaumualii, the crafty king of the island who had been forced to pledge his allegiance five years earlier to Kamehameha I. The crewmembers returned to Sitka aboard another ship and reported their loss.

Alexander Baranov, manager of the Russian American Company, dismissed a plan to invade Kauai and instead dispatched Georg Anton Scheffer to the island in order to find a diplomatic solution to the problem. Scheffer, a German doctor fluent in English, arrived on the Big Island in November 1815 to ask Kamehameha for assistance in getting his company's cargo released.

Kamehameha offered no help and Scheffer decided to negotiate directly with Kaumualii. They worked out a secret treaty in which Scheffer got back the cargo in return for a promise of Russian help if Kaumualii ever decided to make war with Kamehameha. Scheffer would use his ships to attack the other islands and, in the event of victory, would be given half of Oahu and all of its sandalwood forests. The fragrant Hawaiian sandalwood, prized by the Chinese for a variety of uses, was a profitable trade item.

On September 12, 1816, Scheffer began supervising a group of Hawaiians in the construction of Fort Elizabeth at Waimea, named after the wife of the Russian emperor, Alexander I. The base of the star-shaped stone walls, which tapered upwards, were up to seventeen feet wide and over twelve feet high. Cannons were placed around the top.

In addition to Fort Elizabeth, Scheffer was allowed to build two simple earthenwork forts in Hanalei. Little trace of either remains today. Fort Alexander, named in honor of the Russian emperor, sat on a hill above Hanalei Bay. Fort Barclay, named after the Russian army general Barclay de Tolly, was built on the bank of the mouth of the Hanalei River.

Scheffer's plan to turn Kauai into a Russian outpost, however, was never realized. When the Russian brig Rurik visited the islands in December, its commander, Lieutenant Otto von Kotzebue, assured Kamehameha that his emperor had no plans to take over Hawaii. Kamehameha subsequently forced Kaumualii to banish the Russians from Kauai and they left on May 8, 1817.

After the Russians had departed the Hawaiian government finished the fort and used it to house a company of local soldiers. Their duties included greeting visiting ships and recognizing royal birthdays with cannon salutes.

The Hawaiian government dismantled the Waimea fort in 1864 and it gradually fell into disrepair. In 1966 the U.S. Department of the Interior designated the remains of Fort Elizabeth as a National Historic Landmark, and in 1970 the site was acquired by the state for a historical park. ■

WAIMEA RIVER (opposite page): The dark ground near the Waimea River bridge marks the spot where Fort Elizabeth once stood. FORT ELIZABETH (above): This painting by Guy Buffet shows what Fort Elizabeth may have looked like during the Russian days. Courtesy of the State Foundation on Culture and the Arts.

Kauai Kilohana

Kauai's greatest treasure is its people. The island's residents, a harmonious blend of many races, are known throughout the state for their good-natured friendliness and hospitality. They also share an obvious love for their beautiful home. This affection for Kauai is one of the main reasons that the Garden Island attracts thousands upon thousands of travelers a year, a large number of them returning to visit again.

The first people to inhabit Kauai, the seafarers who arrived in their double-hulled canoes fifteen hundred years ago, built a foundation for one of the Pacific's great cultures. They were a strong and hardworking people, religious in spirit, and devoted to their families.

After the discovery of the islands by Captain Cook, the Hawaiians began to share their paradise with other peoples. Westerners comprised the first great wave of outsiders or haoles, a Hawaiian word that today still refers to Caucasians. First ashore were the adventurers who jumped ship, took native wives, and aligned themselves with various chiefs. Then came businessmen looking for new ways to make money and missionaries ready to introduce literacy and Christianity.

Gradually the westerners took over economic control of the islands. In the mid-1800s, they started sugar plantations and hired Hawaiians to cultivate the fields. This was the beginning of the work-for-pay system in Kauai. Since these laborers now had wages to spend as they pleased, the common people gained a sense of independence from the powerful chiefs who had once taken as taxes most of their farm and fishing production.

Rapid expansion of the island sugar industry, however, eventually outstripped the

availability of local Hawaiian workers. The plantation owners then began to recruit laborers from other ethnic backgrounds.

The first Chinese laborers stepped off their ships from Hong Kong in 1852. In 1868 a small group of 148 immigrant workers arrived from Japan and were assimilated quickly into the plantation program. Seventeen years later, in 1885, the first government-sponsored Japanese contract laborers were brought to Hawaii and many were put to work on Kauai's eight sugar plantations.

Other groups also added significantly to the sugar communities on Kauai. Portuguese workers arrived in 1878, Germans in 1881, Puerto Ricans in 1900, Koreans in 1903, and Filipinos in 1906. These were later joined by other peoples, each of whom made—and still make—important contributions to the cosmopolitan culture of Kauai.

The faces of present-day Kauai are a lasting reflection of these immigrant groups who, over the past two centuries, came to the Hawaiian Islands eager to turn their dreams for a better life into reality. Studies show that more than a quarter of the people who now inhabit the island boast of mixed ethnic origins. History has given Kauai a proud, multihued population. ■

CANOE CLUB (opposite page): Members of the Kaiola Canoe Club get together after a race. KIMONO DOLL (above): A young girl wears her kimono during Kauai's annual Prince Kuhio Festival.

HULA TROUPE (right): Members of a male halau hula, or hula school, await their turn to dance. KEEPING WATCH (above): A woman in the audience observes the hula performance.

43

PLUMERIA LEI (opposite page): A child in Lihue wears
a lei of plumeria flowers and a woven palm-frond hat.
SUNDAY MUUMUU (above left): This young girl wears
her muumuu on a Sunday outing in Wailua. YOUNG
BOY (above): The faces of Kauai represent a
mixture of many ethnic groups.

45

46

IN THE PINK (opposite page left): A little girl wears her
pink dress to a Coco Palms wedding ceremony. MISS
HAWAII (opposite page right): Haunani Asing Marston,
a former Miss Hawaii, lives in Hanalei. BIG SMILE
(above): Although missing a front tooth this young lady
manages a friendly smile.

47

KOLOA FARMER (above): This Kauai pig farmer sits in front of his house in Koloa. He supplies pork to several of Kauai's best stores and restaurants.

RANGE RIDERS (above): Many children on Kauai learn to ride early. These two youngsters are grazing their horse at a mountain pasture in Kokee.

49

HANALEI PIER: The pier at Hanalei Bay was originally built in 1912 to help with the unloading of cargo ships. Now used for recreation, it is a reminder of years past when most people and supplies arrived at Hanalei by sea.

52

UNCLE JACK (above): Retired Princeville Ranch paniolo, one
of the main characters in the Disney film "Castaway Cowboy."
BOYS AND CANOES (right): These youngsters are
members of a canoe club in Hanalei.

54

The Mythical Menehune

Waimea Canyon is deserted now but there is evidence of very early habitation. Hand-built walls still stand and petroglyphs have been found carved in the rocks. Some traditions say that Kauai's thick forested canyons and valleys were home to the menehune, a physically short and mischievous people—much like Ireland's beloved leprechauns—that have become a fanciful part of the island's folklore.

While archaeologists have never found the remains of a distinctly small race of ancient people on Kauai, the menehune legends might have a basis in fact. Some scholars now believe that the early Tahitians gave the name "menehune" to the Marquesan people who had reached the islands before them. Perhaps the more powerful Tahitians forced their predecessors into servitude, driving them back into the canyons and valleys. The word "manahune" can be translated as "slave" in the Tahitian language.

Kauai's mythical menehune were a very clever and industrious tribe. They had a reputation as master builders but, for some reason, worked only at night under the glow of the moon. If they could not finish a given task in a single night they abandoned it forever. Fortunately, this occurred only rarely.

During one of their more productive nights the menehune built the island's largest aquaculture reservoir, the Alekoko Fishpond, for a Kauai prince and princess. Located outside Lihue, this mullet-raising pond was created by constructing a nine-hundred-foot dam to cut off an elbow bend in the wide Huleia River. Holes in the dam allow young fish to enter the pond from the river but are too small to allow the grown fish to escape.

A favorite engineering method was to pass rocks by hand along a double row of men in long lines from the site of their quarry. It took exact planning and well-organized teamwork. Before building the Alekoko Fishpond, the menehune warned their royal patrons not to watch the construction that night. Their curiosity got the better of them, though, and they were immediately turned into rock. The two stone pillars are still visible on a nearby hillside.

The little people also get credit for building a number of heiau along the Wailua River and the Menehune Ditch in Waimea. Although the ditch appears quite ordinary on first sight, inspection of the waterway reveals a unique kind of fitted and faced stonework that has been found nowhere else in Hawaii. Only a tiny portion of the ditch has been preserved but it once stretched for miles, starting from a dam upstream of Waimea River and running down the cliff to the farms below.

Legend relates that the ditch was built by the menehune at the request of Ola, a king who wanted to irrigate his taro patches. For their effort on his behalf, Ola gave them a giant feast in their honor featuring dishes of fresh shrimp, their favorite food. A bronze plaque now marks the existing section of causeway where today's island children enjoy sailing their toy canoes upon the miniature river.

Old stories say there were once over a half million menehune living on Kauai. Gradually they went into hiding and disappeared. A census taken in the early 1800s discovered that sixty-five people living in the town of Wainiha on the northern coast of Kauai put down "menehune" as their nationality. This is the last known official report of their existence, although every once in a while island hikers still claim to have seen them scampering about deep within the dark forests. ■

MENEHUNE FISHPOND (opposite page): Alekoko Fishpond, often called the Menehune Fishpond, is located near Nawiliwili Harbor outside Lihue.
MENEHUNE DITCH (above): The Menehune Ditch in Waimea was once used to irrigate taro patches.

Paniolos: Cowboys in Hawaii

It is sometimes startling to see cowboys riding along the edge of Waimea Canyon or riding bulls at a rodeo in Hanalei. An unknowing observer might imagine these events are taking place in Wyoming or Texas, but the tropical beaches and the swaying palm trees identify such familiar scenes as pure Hawaiian.

The ancient Polynesians, of course, did not bring cattle with them on their voyaging canoes. Cows were then unknown in the isolated Pacific islands. It was not until 1793 that the first cattle were brought to the Sandwich Islands by British Captain George Vancouver aboard a sloop-of-war.

These cattle were hardy longhorns, then the major breed in California and Mexico. Vancouver told Kamehameha that the cattle were raised for food but that he should allow time for them to multiply. The king responded by placing a kapu, or restriction, on his gifts for ten years. During that time the cattle were allowed to roam free and protected.

Horses were introduced in 1803 by Richard Cleveland who landed them from an American trading ship. Because they were not to be eaten, Kamehameha did not appreciate the horses as much as the cattle. Most of the early horses brought to the islands were the same wild mustangs that served the cowboys so well in the American Southwest.

The kingdom's uncontrolled cattle population began to cause havoc in the 1820s. Unchecked, the hungry animals had stripped bare most of their original grazing lands and began attacking the farmlands.

Kamehameha III acted to solve the problem in 1832 when he sent an ambassador to California to recruit Spanish-Mexican vaqueros who could teach Hawaiians how to ride and rope. Several cowboys were brought to the islands and became known as paniolos, the local pronun- ciation of espanoles or Spaniards.

Hawaii's native paniolos first copied the flamboyant dress of the vaqueros but, in time, they created their own distinctive image. They rode the range in colorful shirts and wore flower leis on their hand-woven palm leaf hats. When they could not afford to buy imported riding gear they carved their own saddles out of island wood and stretched rawhide over the frames.

Cattle ranching came to Kauai in 1831. Richard Charlton, then British consul in the Hawaiian Islands, took out a twenty-year lease on land between Kilauea and Hanalei and ran a herd of about one hundred head of cattle. Soon, other ranch operations followed and in 1848 the registration of brands was started on Kauai.

One of Kauai's finest herds was kept along the Wailua River by Deborah Kapule, the favorite wife of the island's ruler, Kaumualii. Through the efforts of Kapule and others, the stock on Kauai was gradually improved, and by the turn of the century there were thousands of top-grade cattle on the island.

Today there are several large cattle ranches on Kauai and hundreds of paniolos who trace their occupational ancestry back to the days of the vaqueros. For them the Garden Island might as well be the Old West. ■

MIRANDA RANCH (opposite page): A horseman rides on the Miranda Ranch in Waimea. WAIMEA COWBOY (above): Jimmy Miranda of Waimea takes part in a local rodeo.

58

CHASING A CALF (above): A youngster practices
the art of calf roping. RANGE MEMORIES (opposite page
left): A veteran paniolo remembers the good old days at Rice
Ranch in Lihue. YOUNG COWBOY (opposite page
right): This Hanalei youngster still has plenty
of memories to acquire.

CALF ROPING (opposite page): Roping calves from the
saddle of a horse is still part of the basic paniolo skills.
CATTLE SKULLS (above): These cattle skulls decorate
the side of a cabin in Kokee. COWBOY HAT (right): A
well-worn cowboy hat hangs within easy reach of its owner.

Koolau the Outlaw

The most famous paniolo in the history of Kauai did not gain his notoriety by merely riding the range. He did it, instead, by contracting leprosy and, resisting government relocation efforts, by battling law officers from his hideout deep within Kalalau Valley.

Koolau the Outlaw was born at Kekaha in 1862. He was educated at Waimea and, like many of his classmates, became a paniolo at the age of seventeen. Legend says he was a talented saddle maker and an excellent shot with a rifle.

In 1881 he married a strong-willed girl named Piilani and two years later their son, Kaleimanu, was born. They set up a comfortable household in a small cottage outside Waimea while Koolau was employed by several cattle ranches in the area.

Everything was fine for the young couple until 1889 when Koolau, and then Kaleimanu, began to develop a skin rash that was eventually diagnosed as leprosy. In those days all leprosy victims in Hawaii were sent to the isolated Kalaupapa colony on Molokai.

Koolau was, at first, willing to go to Molokai. The health authorities had promised that Piilani could accompany him and their son to the colony. When they changed their minds, he changed his. Grabbing his rifle and camp gear the young paniolo saddled his horses and rode with his wife and young son up into Kokee. From there they hiked on foot into Kalalau Valley.

Upon reaching Kalalau, the family met a band of about two dozen other lepers who were living in the valley. They told Koolau that they would die fighting rather than be forced to go to Molokai.

News of Koolau's dramatic escape spread across the island, and government officials realized that such defiance could not be ignored. The original plan was to organize a large posse, but Kauai Deputy Sheriff Louis H. Stoltz decided preparations were going too slowly.

In June 1893 the deputy was dropped off alone on the beach and he hiked into Kalalau Valley. Searching near the hideout of the lepers he was confronted by Koolau. A fight resulted—it is not clear what exactly happened—and Koolau killed Stoltz with a couple of rifle shots to the stomach.

The death of the deputy sheriff angered government officials. Koolau was no longer just an innocent victim of leprosy. He had become an outlaw. At the end of July an armed force, consisting of a dozen policemen and fourteen National Guard soldiers, took a steamer from Honolulu.

Once ashore the policemen and soldiers began rounding up the lepers. All were captured except Koolau, who had taken up a protected position on a flat ledge overlooking a steep trail. The government troops assaulted the ledge but Koolau killed two of the men with rifle bursts.

In the midst of the confusion Koolau escaped. The troops gave up the chase and returned to Honolulu. A $1000 reward was offered but it was never collected. The family held out until 1896, the year both Koolau and his son died. Piilani buried them in the valley and returned to Waimea.

Over the years the adventures of Koolau have become part of the island's folklore. Jack London popularized the legend in his fictional story, "Koolau the Leper," which was included in his 1916 book, House of Pride. Today some hikers make special trips into Kalalau Valley just to see the places associated with the legendary outlaw. ■

RICE RANCH (opposite page): Cowboys head off to check the cattle at Rice Ranch. OUTLAW HIDEAWAY (above): Kalalau Valley was the hideout of Koolau, a Waimea cowboy who contracted Hansen's Disease in the 1890's and fought against efforts to deport him to the leper colony on Molokai.

64

Rural America, Paradise Style

Kauai may be contemporary in outlook but progress has not affected its old-fashioned country charm. Despite modern airports and luxury hotels, Kauai is still largely a rural island, full of farms and small towns, of wooden churches and neighborhood schools. Family businesses are common to the Garden Island, and many of the retail shops have served their customers in the same location for generations.

The fourth largest island in the Hawaiian chain, Kauai is roughly circular in shape and occupies an area of 549.4 square miles. The 1980 census put the population of Kauai at thirty-nine thousand, which is only about four percent of the total for the entire state. Kauai County, which includes the island of Niihau, is one of four counties in Hawaii.

Lihue, the county seat, started out in the 1850s as a village tied to the Lihue Plantation and Grove Farm. Today it is the island's major town and a busy government and commercial center. Because it was born in the age of the automobile, Lihue is visibly different in scale from the rest of the island. Its wider streets are designed for heavier traffic and the buildings are larger and more permanent.

Although possessing its own sense of history, Lihue is a relative newcomer when compared to other towns on the island. Waimea, where Captain Cook landed in 1778, was the most heavily populated section of the island through the early 1800s. The fertile land in the area encouraged agriculture and the Waimea River was easily fished.

Hanapepe stepped into the spotlight around the turn of this century. The island's Asian immigrants introduced rice farming to the valley, and tons of rice were harvested each year by area farmers. The town's Japanese and Chinese merchants also supported themselves through trade with the thousands of plantation workers. Port Allen and Burns Field, the island's primary airport during the 1920s, were both located at Hanapepe.

In 1913 the Kauai County Building was dedicated in Lihue and it is now the oldest continuously occupied county building in the state. The A.S. Wilcox Memorial Library (now the Kauai Museum), built in 1924, was another town anchor.

Construction on the deepwater Nawiliwili Harbor, near Lihue, began in 1924 and was finished in 1930. It offered better protection from stormy weather than Port Allen and was closer to Oahu. Lihue further established itself as Kauai's primary town in 1939 when it was linked up to the new Belt Road that wrapped around the coast.

Through the 1970s and early 1980s sugar continued to dominate the island economy and lifestyle. Thousands of cane acres stretched shore to shore. In recent years, however, the sugar business has fallen into decline and tourism has become an important factor in the island's continued economic growth. This rise of tourism now offers travelers the best of two worlds. Kauai's visitors can not only stay at first class hotels and dine at fine restaurants, they can also experience a slice of rural America that just happens to be tucked away in paradise. ■

COMMUNITY CHURCH (opposite page): The Baptist church in Anahola was originally built by sugar plantation workers. TIRE SWING (above): A young boy swings on a tire from a tree in Makaweli.

HONORING HER PAST (left): A fern-draped hula student waits for her chance to dance in the manner of her ancestors. CHILD WITH LEI (above): This young girl wears a lei of pink plumeria flowers. PROUD PANIOLO (opposite page): The original paniolos in Hawaii learned the art of cattle ranching from imported Mexican cowboys.

68

WAINIHA BRIDGE (above): This youngster
rides his bicycle across the Wainiha River Bridge
near his home. PASTURE LANDS (right): Horses graze
peacefully under palm trees in upper Wailua. SUGAR
PLANTER (far right): A woman in Koloa uses a
digging pole to plant sugar cane.

69

TALKING STORY (above left): A woman leans over her fence to talk with neighbors at Koloa Plantation. TRUCK STOP (above): This woman waits with her son for the school bus in Waimea.

SMOKING GARDENER (above): While watering the plants outside her house on Numila Plantation this woman enjoys an afternoon cigar.

71

72

STONE CHURCH (above): Christ Memorial Church
in Kilauea was built of lava rocks in 1941. The stained
glass windows were imported from England.
PLANTATION PORCH (right): Riding gear sits on the
front porch of this Hanalei plantation home.

HANAPEPE BUILDING (above): Kauai has numerous
old buildings like this one that were built during the
plantation era.

76

GRANDFATHER (above): Arthur Palama of Kokee
holds his grandchildren. TARO FIELDS (right): This family
taro farm is located in Wainiha.

78

Sugar is the Life of the Land

Sugarcane is not native to Hawaii. It was introduced to the islands by the first Polynesian settlers. When Captain Cook arrived at Kauai in 1778, he found several varieties of sugarcane already growing here. He noted in his logbook that the cane was "of large size and good quality."

Cook described the cane fields he saw as "plantations," but that is not quite true. The Hawaiians grew the tall stalks primarily as wind breaks and hedges between their garden plots. They did not process any sugar but merely chewed the stalk for its sweet juice.

During the early 1800s a number of individuals started small sugar operations in Hawaii but none was especially successful. Hawaii's first successful sugar plantation operation began on Kauai in 1835 when three ambitious young men from New England obtained a lease from Kamehameha III for 980 acres of land at Koloa. William Ladd, William Hooper, and Peter Allan Brinsmade picked a tract that included a mill location near Maulili Waterfall that could be dammed and used for power. Their lease was for fifty years with an annual rent of $300.

Ladd and Company, harvested its first sugarcane in 1837—1838. The company's yield was thirty tons of sugar and 170 barrels of molasses. Koa tree logs, arranged vertically, were first used as grinding rollers until iron rollers became available. In setting up the Koloa plantation, Hooper established a general store and dairy, and provided housing and gardening plots for the Hawaiian workers. Medical assistance was provided by a missionary doctor.

When the structures at Maulili became inadequate for the expanding plantation, the owners built a bigger mill in 1841 on a site at Waihohonu. Workers' quarters were enclosed by a stone wall that completely surrounded the five-acre site. This new mill processed about forty carts of sugarcane each day.

Koloa prospered around Ladd and Company, later known as Koloa Plantation. It became the agricultural center of Kauai and one of the island's most active communities. Each year between forty and sixty ships of all kinds anchored at Koloa Landing, a stone pier built a few miles away at the mouth of Koloa Stream.

In 1913 a new Koloa mill was built in Paa, a mile east of the outdated Koloa facilities. World War II brought labor shortages and maintenance difficulties for the aging factory and in 1948 the Koloa Plantation was bought and absorbed by Grove Farm. Since 1974, the factory and Koloa's still productive sugarcane fields have been leased by McBryde Sugar Company, Limited.

Today only the remains of the 1841 boiling house and stone smokestack survive. In 1985 the 150th anniversary of the local sugar industry was celebrated in Koloa with the dedication of a large monument and bronze sculpture near the old mill ruins.

Old Koloa Town, the renovated commercial center of the community, is now an attractive shopping complex that consists of historic vintage buildings—the oldest dating from 1898—that have been linked together by pedestrian walkways and landscaped courtyards. Kauai's pioneering sugar town, once the economic hub of the Garden Island, has come alive again. ■

PLANTATION TRUCK (opposite page): A loaded truck leaves the Koloa Sugar Mill. SUGAR CANE (above): Sugar cane stalks sway in the wind at Koloa.

Sun, Sand, and Sea

Kauai is an outdoors island. Its beaches attract sunbathers and its mountains attract hikers. Fishermen rave about its surrounding waters and golfers love to play on its championship courses. For other residents and visitors the island stirs up visions of camping, horseback riding, and scuba diving.

Beaches, of course, are the pride of tropical islands and Kauai is famous for its miles of sandy shoreline. Some of its beaches are known as far away as Hollywood; others are local secrets, hidden away, down narrow backcountry roads. It is not unusual to find a favorite beach that's practically deserted.

The western side of the island, starting back from the end of the road at Polihale, is a warm coastal stretch marked by wide sandy beaches. Polihale State Park, between Na Pali Coast and Barking Sands, has one of the finest beaches in the state. There are picnic and camping facilities at the park.

Barking Sands, part of the U.S. Pacific Missile Test Range Facility, is open to the public and takes its name from a large sand dune that is 60 feet high and a half-mile long. During dry seasons the dune emits a distinct "woofing" sound when people slide down its steep banks. Another lovely spot along this coast is located at Kekaha Beach Park. Camping is not permitted here but the long beach is perfect for swimming, sunbathing, and building sandcastles.

The shoreline from Lawai to Poipu is sometimes called Kauai's "Gold Coast." It is known for its mild dry weather, friendly lifestyle, and excellent beaches. A few years back, the area was fairly sleepy but today, with the addition of new luxury resort hotels at Poipu, the best beaches draw crowds on the sunny weekends.

For quieter pleasures the coast road continues past Brennecke's Beach and leads to remote Shipwreck Beach. This small sandy beach, surrounded by rocky terrain, recalls the sinking of a fishing boat. Driftwood and seashells can be gathered along the beach and secluded coves.

Continuing past Lihue the windward side of the island is exposed to pleasant tradewinds. There are good beaches from Kalapaki to Kapaa Beach Park, especially in the Lydgate Park area favored by the ancient royalty of Kauai. Across the Wailua River bridge there are still more beaches fronting the oceanside resort hotels in Kapaa.

Down the road at Anahola Beach Park there is a fine sandy beach and clean calm water for swimming. Anahola Bay curves gracefully from Kahala Point to Kuaehu Point and then inward toward the scenic background of the Makaleha Mountains. From here the road bends around the northeast corner of the island.

Just beyond Kilauea is Kalihiwai Bay. This sheltered bay is popular with local folks on weekends but fairly uncrowded on weekdays. A half-mile away is Anini Beach Park, where camping is permitted, and then the resort community of Princeville, a key attraction for tennis players and golfers.

One of the most photographed beaches on the island is Lumahai, off the road between Hanalei Bay and Haena. There is end-of-the-road parking at Haena's Kee Beach which is fine for swimming and snorkeling. From here the foot-trail leads along Na Pali Coast back to Kalalau Valley. Hikers along the route can take their pick from miles of unspoiled beaches and some of the most magnificent scenery Kauai has to offer. ■

WAIPOULI BEACH (opposite page): Waipouli Beach, between Wailua and Kapaa, is deserted early in the morning. BATHING BEAUTY (above): An attractive young lady takes in the sun at Poipu Beach Park.

*WAINIHA BAY (opposite page): This grass hunting shack
sits on a sand bar in Wainiha Bay. LANDING CANOES
(above): Members of an island canoe club push their
canoes into the water near Kapaa.*

83

POLIHALE STATE PARK: *The wide beach at Polihale stretches several miles from Barking Sands (a military beach enjoyed by the public) to the dramatic cliffs that mark the beginning of Napili Coast State Park.*

TUNNELS BEACH (above): A fisherman prepares a sling
for spear fishing along Tunnels Beach near Haena.
SPOUTING HORN (right): The spouting horn at Poipu
explodes as sea water splashes out of a shoreline lava tube.

BARKING SANDS *(above): A four-wheel vehicle, loaded
down with surfboards, crosses the dunes at Barking Sands.
This is the longest continual beach in the islands.*

ON THE BEACH (*above*): *A mother and child enjoy a sunny day at Hanalei Bay.* RIDING SUNSET (*right*): *Horseback riders end their day with a romantic detour along the beach at Waimea.*

ANAHOLA BAY (above): Campers make weekend home
at Anahola Beach Park along Anahola Bay.

89

KAYAK PADDLING (above): A kayak paddler passes
Anini Beach near Princeville. POIPU BEACH (right): Perfect
weather is taken for granted along beautiful Poipu Beach.

Gardens Full of Flowers

Kauai carries its "Garden Island" nickname well. To begin with, the sunny climate and heavy mountain rainfall encourages a natural abundance of flowers and lush tropical vegetation. Local residents have, in turn, responded to these factors by developing a number of outstanding cultivated gardens.

Each of the Hawaiian Islands has its own symbolic flower. For Kauai it is the native mokihana, a flower that grows on a bush-like tree that belongs to the citrus family. It is found only in the forests of Kauai. The plant has small green flowers and fragrant seed pods which are often strung into leis with maile leaves.

Kauai's oldest and most historic formal garden is Lawai Kai, the private one-hundred-acre estate of Kauai architect John Gregg Allerton located in Lawai Valley. The gardens here were started by Queen Emma, wife of Kamehameha IV, in the 1870s. A cottage built for Queen Emma, now a registered National Historic Landmark, has been preserved on the property.

The adjacent Pacific Tropical Botanical Garden, a conservation project supported by the Allerton family, is located on 186 acres upstream from their estate. Although chartered by the U.S. Congress in 1964, it remains privately funded by a number of individuals, foundations, and corporations.

At the present time the Pacific Tropical Botanical Garden maintains two satellite gardens, a 125-acre site near Hana, Maui, and a large 1,000-acre-preserve in Limahuli Valley on the northern coast of Kauai. Limahuli Valley receives heavier rainfall than Lawai Valley and its lush forest area contains several newly discovered species of rare, native Hawaiian plants.

Smith's Tropical Paradise, formerly Paradise Pacifica, is located on thirty acres that border the Wailua River. Its thousands of trees and plants are set in a tropical garden that contains a waterfall, large lily ponds, and thatched houses that recall the ancient days when Hawaiians built their villages on the river banks.

Menehune Garden, in Nawiliwili, is also named after Kauai's legendary little people. These attractive grounds, planted and maintained for many years by the Kailikea family, are especially noted for a wide variety of native plants that were utilized by the early Hawaiians.

Kiahuna Gardens in Poipu was begun in 1938 to house the extensive cactus specimens grown by Hector Moir, then owner of the Koloa Plantation and a worldwide plant collector. Legends indicate this property was once the location of a temple used to train hula dancers. Today this piece of land is incorporated into the beautifully planted grounds of the Kiahuna Plantation.

Olu Pua Botanical Garden and Plantation, at Kalaheo, used to be the estate garden for the manager of the Kauai Pineapple Plantation. Set on twelve acres it was begun in 1932 when the main house was built and carefully cultivated until the plantation closed in 1962. Still privately owned, Olu Pua contains a number of theme gardens featuring colorful ornamental plants. According to one translator, the name of Olu Pua means "feeling pleasant in a garden of flowers." Such a poetic phrase could easily refer to all of Kauai. Paradise has found a home on the Garden Island. ■

ALLERTON GARDENS (opposite page): The Allerton estate at Lawai Kai was developed on property that originally belonged to Queen Emma, the wife of Kamehameha IV. It is now a part of the Pacific Tropical Botanical Garden. RED GINGER (above): Red ginger blooms at Olu Pua Gardens.

PHILODENDRON (opposite page): These plants glisten after a rainfall at the Fern Grotto. FERN GROTTO (above): The Fern Grotto, located on the Wailua River, is the mouth of a lava tube cave surrounded by feathery ferns. CHINESE 'APE (right): These plants are at Olu Pua Gardens.

96

WATER LILIES (above): Water Lilies burst forth in the
Gardens at Kiahuna Plantation. LILY POND (right):
These lily ponds are in the Pacific Tropical Botanical
Gardens. GINGER BLOSSOM (far right): Wild
ginger at Pacific Tropical Botanical Gardens.

PASSION FLOWER (opposite page): This passion
flower blooms in Kokee. HIBISCUS (opposite page right):
The hibiscus is the official state flower. JATROPHA
(above): This flower blooms at Pacific
Tropical Botanical Gardens.

EUCALYPTUS AVENUE (opposite page): Kauai's tall tunnel of eucalyptus trees folds its branches over the road to Koloa. STRAWBERRY BANANA (above left): This strawberry banana grows at the Pacific Tropical Botanical Gardens. BANANA PLANT: A young banana plant at Pacific Tropical Botanical Garden.

PALM FROND *(above): This palm frond catches
the sun at Olu Pua Gardens.* COCONUT GROVE
*(opposite page): This grove of coconut trees is on the
grounds of the Coco Palms Hotel.*

Hollywood Moves to Kauai

Movie audiences and television viewers are accustomed to seeing Kauai on the screen. Over thirty major Hollywood motion pictures, hit television shows, and mini-series have been shot on the Garden Island. Its tropical beauty, sunny weather, and varied scenic locations make it a great favorite of film directors.

The romance between movie makers and Kauai began decades ago. Pagan Love Song, a 1950 movie starring Esther Williams, was shot on location there, set, as was the popular 1951 film Bird of Paradise, with Jeff Chandler and Debra Paget. The present Chapel in the Palms on the grounds of the Coco Palms Hotel was originally built for the 1954 movie Miss Sadie Thompson featuring Rita Hayworth and Jose Ferrer.

James A. Michener created Bali Hai out of pure imagination for his Pulitzer Prize-winning story collection Tales of the South Pacific. When the book was turned into the 1958 movie musical, however, Kauai was substituted for Michener's fictional island. Much of South Pacific, starring Rossano Brazzi and Mitzi Gaynor, was shot around Hanalei.

Elvis Presley made three movies in Hawaii during the 1960s: Blue Hawaii (1961), Girls! Girls! Girls! (1963) and Paradise Hawaiian Style (1966). All included bits of scenic footage shot on Kauai.

In 1975 the island sequences for the remake of King Kong, starring Jessica Lange, was shot by Dino DeLaurentiis at Honopu on Kauai's Na Pali Coast. A year later George C. Scott sailed down the broad Wailua River (supposedly in the Florida Keys) in the 1976 film adaptation of Ernest Hemingway's novel Islands in the Stream. In 1979 the Allerton estate in Lawai Kai was used for the mission station in Disney's The Last Flight of Noah's Ark, starring Elliott Gould and Genevieve Bujold. The background of Kauai was transformed into South America for the opening scenes of Raiders of the Lost Ark (1980) and into Vietnam rice paddies for Uncommon Valor (1983).

Television viewers saw much of the islands in "Hawaii Five-0," which brightened the tube from 1967 to 1980. Many of the

Neighbor Island scenes were shot on Kauai. When Jack Lord retired from his lead role as Steve McGarrett he handed over the detective work to Tom Selleck who skyrocketed to fame playing Thomas Magnum in "Magnum P.I." Most of the action takes place on Oahu but Magnum's pal, T. C., often flies his helicopter to Kauai for Neighbor Island episodes.

Another television show that has used Kauai in recent years is "Fantasy Island." Wailua Falls can be seen under the opening credits and "Fantasy Island" aerial sequences are often filmed along Na Pali Coast. Kauai doubled for Australia in "The Thorn Birds," a 1983 television mini-series that starred Richard Chamberlain, Rachel Ward, and Barbara Stanwyck.

Haena became Matlock Island for the mini-series, an Australian island close to the Great Barrier Reef. Meggie's beach in the program, where Father Ralph de Bricassart (played by Chamberlain) and Meggie Cleary (played by Ward) have their most romantic scenes together is actually Kee Beach.

Dungloe Village in North Queensland, Australia, was actually Hanapepe, a town whose older section still retains the look of the 1930s. Koloa Sugar Mill, one of four still in operation on Kauai, was also portrayed. The plantation was called Himmelhoch in the series, and that name can still be seen painted on one side of the mill. ■

BEACH HOUSE (opposite page): The Allerton House above Kee Beach was used as a background location in "The Thorn Birds" television mini-series. LUMAHAI BEACH (above): Lumahai Beach was known as Nurses Beach in the film version of South Pacific.

It's Still Yesterday in Hanalei

The past meets the present at Hanalei and, despite their differences, somehow they manage to get along in relative harmony. Life seems less serious here, more gentle and relaxed. The dreamy pace of this tropical beach town is a reminder of how the rest of the island looked during the first part of this century.

Hanalei has long been a treasured place to the people of Kauai. During ancient times the Hawaiians had a major village here, clustered around the picturesque bay, and there were a number of individual homesteads located back in the valleys. Fishing and farming bonded the people into a tight-knit community.

After the missionaries arrived in 1834 the door opened slightly to the outside world, but changes were still slow to come. Interisland sailing ships made periodic stops at Hanalei but the harbor could be hazardous to larger vessels, especially during the stormy winter months. When the sea lanes were closed, the supplies came in by foot or horseback over the narrow dirt road that connected the North Shore to Wailua.

Today this same road is paved beneath a steady stream of cars; but the view from the Hanalei Valley Lookout, on the edge of town, has probably stayed much the same. Visitors still hold their breath while looking out on the dramatic panorama that spreads out over the taro fields to the distant mountains. A portion of Hanalei Valley is a federal wildlife refuge for endangered birds.

Drivers heading into town must first cross the gateway to Hanalei, a one-lane steel truss bridge that was built in 1912. The oldest bridge of this type now left in the state, it has come to symbolize the slower lifestyle of the area's residents. The narrow bridge blocks heavy trucks and buses that have invaded the rest of the island.

Hanalei itself has kept the spirit of a South Seas outpost. One plantation-era building even houses the Tahiti Nui Bar, so named by its owners because Hanalei reminded them more of their home, Tahiti. Its front porch is a favorite spot for cool drinks in the late afternoon. Other town highlights include a couple of general stores, boutiques and rental shops, restaurants, gas pumps, and a combination museum/snack bar.

The nine-mile drive from Hanalei to Haena is as scenic as any on Kauai. Colorful wildflowers bloom beneath the trees and forest birds are often heard singing overhead. Past Lumahai Beach of *South Pacific* fame is the tiny community of Wainiha, the final dwelling place of the people who called themselves menehune.

Across the road from Haena Beach Park is Maniniholo Dry Cave, actually the opening of a lava tube named after a great menehune fisherman. Farther ahead are the Waikapalae and Waikanaloa Wet Caves, both linked to the goddess Pele.

Local residents never pass this way without looking up to the mountains toward a large boulder perched on a rounded peak. This rock is called Pohaku-O-Kane, "the rock of Kane." It is said that when this rock falls the island of Kauai will begin sinking back into the ocean. ∎

HANALEI VALLEY (opposite page): Food plants have been raised in the fertile Hanalei Valley since ancient times. HANALEI PIER (above): Fishermen cast their lines off the pier at Hanalei Bay.

STEEL BRIDGE (above): This steel truss bridge was built in 1912. It is the oldest remaining bridge of its type in the state. HANALEI TARO (opposite page): A view across the taro fields toward Hanalei.

TAHITI NUI BAR (opposite page): Louise Marston sits on the front porch of her Tahiti Nui Bar in Hanalei.
WAINIHA VALLEY (above): Youngsters walk along a road in Wainiha Valley. PICKING TARO (above): Taro is still collected by hand in Hanalei.

111

TARO FARMING: *The Koga family harvests taro from its patches in Hanalei Valley. Kauai has two factories which process the island's taro into poi.*

114

HANALEI BAY *(above): Hanalei Bay and its pier are
illuminated by the evening light.*

PRINCEVILLE (above): Princeville is a planned resort
community on Kauai's north shore.

116

CATAMARANS (above): Catamarans are rigged and ready to sail at Hanalei Beach Park. ABOVE HANALEI (right): Red bougainvilleas add a touch of color to this hillside view of Hanalei Bay.

CANOE RACING (above): Paddlers cruise down
the Hanalei River.

FROM THE PIER (*opposite page*): *Hanalei Bay as seen*
from the pier. SURFING AT HANALEI (*above*): *A surfer*
catches a wave at Hanalei Bay.

BALI HAI: *Lumahai Beach, near Hanalei, was one of
the major sets for the 1958 movie musical, South Pacific.
This sandy spot was called Nurses Beach in the film.*

BEGIN THE DANCE (above): The sound of a conch shell
begins a hula performance at Kee Beach. BALI HAI (above
right): Surfers catch the waves beneath the mountain peak
identified as Bali Hai in the movie "South Pacific."

HANALEI SUNSET (above): Hanalei is a place
without time and schedules.

Spreading the Good Word

The brig Thaddeus sailing from Boston, arrived at the Big Island village of Kailua on April 4, 1820. Aboard were the first Christian missionaries to reach the Hawaiian Islands, dispatched by the American Board of Commissioners for Foreign Missions. The organization had been formed a decade earlier by the Congregational Churches of New England.

Included in this first missionary party were seven men, their wives, and five children. Only two of the men were ordained ministers. Reverend Asa Thurston and his wife were given permission to stay in Kailua, the residence of the king, while the rest of the group continued on to Honolulu with Reverend Hiram Bingham and his wife. The mission headquarters was eventually established there.

By the end of July 1820, two of the missionary couples, Samuel and Mercy Whitney and Samuel and Nancy Ruggles, had moved to Kauai where they settled in Waimea. At the start they lived in a thatched grass house but soon began to construct the kind of home they had left far behind in New England. When completed the next year this was the first Western-style structure erected on Kauai.

The large building sat on a slope above the Waimea River and below the old Russian fort. It had a kitchen, dining area, five bedrooms, and meeting rooms for church activities and school classes. Between sixty and seventy children attended the mission school.

Over the next several decades the missionaries were joined by further companies from New England, and they began to branch out into other parts of the islands. A second Kauai mission station was established at Hanalei in 1834 and a third at Koloa in 1835. In each case the hardworking New Englanders took local materials and used them to construct houses and churches. Their structures had pitched roofs, projecting eaves, and wide lanais—architectural features still present on island buildings.

The Waioli Mission Station was founded in Hanalei at the request of the Hawaiians. Reverend William P. Alexander and his wife, Mary Ann, sailed around the island from Waimea in a double-hulled canoe. For two years they lived in a native hut, then in 1837 constructed the still-standing Waioli Mission House. The frame of the house was made of local ohia wood but the siding was imported from the mainland northwest. Cut coral blocks were used for the chimney.

In 1841 the Alexanders and a Hawaiian crew built the Waioli Church. Seven acres of sugarcane were sold to pay for the new structure, the first Christian church constructed on Kauai's north shore. It was an impressive structure for its time and is now viewed as a perfect blend of Hawaiian and Western architecture. Waioli Church soon became the focal point of the Hanalei community.

William Alexander was transferred to Maui in 1834 and a few years later Abner and Lucy Wilcox, missionary teachers from Connecticut, took over the residence. The Wilcoxes lived in the house from 1846 until they died on a trip back to New England in 1869. They raised eight sons in Hanalei, including George N. Wilcox, who took over the Grove Farm sugar plantation in 1864.

The small roadside Waioli Huiia Congregational Church, with its attractive high-vaulted roof and stained glass windows, was built in 1912 to replace the original Waioli Church. The old church became the present Waioli Mission Hall.

In 1921 the Mission House and Mission Hall were restored in memory of Abner and Lucy Wilcox by three of their grandchildren. Etta Wilcox Sloggett and Elsie and Mabel Wilcox hired noted Honolulu architect Hart Wood for the job. Three decades later, in 1952, the house was officially incorporated as a museum and opened to the public. Today the Waioli Mission House Museum, with its period furniture and antiques, provides a fascinating peek into Hanalei's historic past. ■

WAIOLI CHURCH (opposite page): The Waioli Huiia Church in Hanalei dates from 1912. In the background is Waioli Social Hall, the original mission church, built in 1841.

126

Na Pali is a Place Apart

Hiking along Kauai's Na Pali Coast, beginning at Kee Beach and ending in Kalalau Valley, is one of the great outdoor experiences in Hawaii. The scenic trail winds up through thick tropical forests, over high cliffs (Na Pali means "the cliffs" in Hawaiian), and down past hauntingly beautiful beaches. For some it represents an escape from civilization, a journey back to those days before the arrival of Captain Cook.

Na Pali Trail, nearly eleven miles long, is basically the same pathway traveled by the ancient Hawaiians. Its use declined after the turn of the present century, but in the mid-1930s sections of it were cleared and restored. The entire length is now maintained by the Division of State Parks, which requires permits for overnight camping.

Beyond Hanalei and Wainiha the north shore road ends at Kee Beach, now part of Haena State Park. From the beach the trail rises steeply for about a mile and then descends another mile to Hanakapiai Valley. It is a pleasant one-hour walk and day hikers usually stop for a picnic near the beach. There is good swimming here, several caves to explore, and camping sites along both sides of the Hanakapiai Stream.

A side trail leads back into the valley to Hanakapiai Falls. This is a fairly strenuous hike of just over a mile and should not be attempted during or after heavy rains. Flash flooding is always a possibility. The waterfall cascades about three hundred feet, in three tiers, down the face of the cliff.

Rising steeply out of Hanakapiai Valley, the trail switches back and forth past two small valleys, Hoolau and Waiahuakua. At some spots the trail, now a thousand feet above sea level, is quite narrow and rock slides have occurred in the past.

Four miles from Hanakapiai is Hanakoa Valley, broadly terraced by the early Hawaiians. Farming here was popular then due to its perfect combination of heavy rainfall and strong sunshine. There are swimming pools along Hanakoa Stream and another waterfall is located in back of the valley.

The most difficult hiking along Na Pali Coast trail is between Hanakoa Valley and Kalalau. Switchbacks are frequent along this

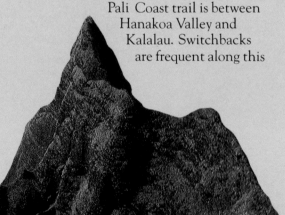

nearly five-mile section which winds over high, mudslide- and rockslide-prone cliffs.

Much of this stretch of trail is across open land that was, until 1975, used for cattle grazing by the Makaweli Ranch, an outfit operated by the same Robinson family which also owns the private island of Niihau. Like the rest of the coastline, this area is now part of the state park system.

Camping in Kalalau Valley is permitted only on the beach, under the trees just back from the beach, and in the shoreline caves on the west side of Kalalau Stream. On the western edge of Kalalau Beach is a huge arched lava rock, three hundred feet long and one hundred-feet high, that projects out into the water. Since it is practically impossible to climb from the beach, most hikers never see the other side. Only a strong and experienced ocean swimmer can make it around the end of the rock to the other side.

Adventurers who succeed will discover several small beaches and the entrance to Honopu Valley. In 1922, a Kauai newspaper editor poetically nicknamed Honopu the "Valley of the Lost Tribe" but there is no scientific basis for such a claim. Legends abound but little archaeological fieldwork has been done in Honopu, the most remote of the valleys on Kauai's spectacular Na Pali Coast. ■

MISTY COASTLINE (opposite page): Na Pali Coast is often wrapped in a blanket of mist.
MOUNTAIN PEAK (above): A pointed sentinel stands guard over Na Pali Coast.

HELICOPTER TOURING (opposite page left): A helicopter flies around Na Pali Coast to give passengers a close-up of its spectacular scenery. ALONG THE TRAIL (opposite page right): Hikers wind their way over the Kalalau Trail. RAFT RIDE (above): A motorized rubber raft takes visitors on a sightseeing trip of Na Pali Coast.

VALLEY VIEW (above): Kalalau Valley has a reputation for harboring hermits, fugitives, and campers anxious to escape the bonds of civilization. EROSION LINES (right): Millions of years of wind and rain have cut deeply into Na Pali Coast. SEA CAVE (far right): A kayaker paddles through a natural arch near Honopu Beach.

131

NA PALI COAST: *A panoramic look down the rugged Na Pali Coast toward Hanalei. This entire stretch of spectacular coastline is now a state park.*

NA PALI BEACHES (above): The beauty of
Na Pali's beaches is enhanced by limited access.
BEHIND NA PALI (opposite page): A view of Na Pali
Coast looking toward the ocean.

KALALAU BEACH (above): The beach at Kalalau has long been a favorite destination of hikers and campers.
HONOPU ARCHWAY (right): The rays of the morning sun shine through the arch at Honopu.

SAND AND SUNSET (above): Sunset ends the day
at Kalalau Beach.

Where Pele Danced

Kauai played an important part in the early history and development of hula. It was at a site overlooking Kee Beach, at the end of the road in Haena, that Pele danced for the high chief, Lohiau. Her performance is central to the "Pele and Hiiaka" legend, the most famous of all Hawaiian epic stories.

The most complete version of the legend is found in the book Pele and Hiiaka, written by Nathaniel B. Emerson and published in 1915. Emerson's work is a compilation of the Pele myths, drawn from previous books, newspapers, and personal interviews.

According to Emerson's account, Pele fell asleep one day on the Big Island while she was listening to the chanting of her younger sister, Hiiaka. In her sleep she heard the sound of drums on Kauai and her spirit-body went to investigate. When Pele's spirit arrived at Kee she found a hula recital in progress.

Pele and Lohiau, one of the drummers, were immediately attracted to each other. After the performance was over they remained together for three days but the spirit refused to make love with the chief. She told him she had to return to the Big Island and would eventually send for him to join her.

Once the spirit goddess had departed, Lohiau grew very depressed. He thought that he would never see Pele again. In a moment of grief he took off his malo, or loincloth, and hung himself from a rafter.

Meanwhile, on the Big Island, Pele awakened from her long sleep with thoughts of Lohiau. She asked Hiiaka if she would travel to Kauai and bring back the handsome young chief. Hiiaka accepted the challenge but during her travels had to defeat a number of evil monsters that attacked her.

Upon arriving on Kauai, Hiiaka learned of the suicide and tracked down the dead man's ghost inside a cave on the island's Na Pali Coast. She finally captured the ghost and forced it back into the body through an eye socket. Lohiau was thus completely restored to life. The pair then returned to the Big Island but fell in love during the homeward journey. Pele's anger over losing Lohiau to her younger sister keeps the volcano fires burning today.

Archaeologists say the Kee site was continually used until the early years of this century. Visitors today will find a trail leading along the shoreline that turns inland toward the high cliffs. The large lava rock structure, consisting of three platforms, is the Kaulu Paoa Heiau or temple. It was named after Paoa, a friend of Lohiau.

On the slope directly above the heiau are a number of narrow terraces. Local tradition says that a halau was once located at this spot. The halau was called Ke-ahu-a-Laka, in honor of Laka, the hula goddess. It was here that the spirit-body of Pele attracted Lohiau with her dancing.

Hula groups from Kauai occasionally used the historic halau terraces for graduation ceremonies through the 1930s but the practice stopped during World War II. In 1983 the sound of the conch shell was heard again and the drums competed with the pounding surf. Now several teachers regularly bring their students here to chant and to dance in hula's most legendary place. ∎

Niihau, the Unreachable Neighbor

The island of Niihau, located eighteen miles southwest of Kauai, is deliberately cut off from the influences of the outside world. For over a century, access has been limited to those Hawaiian families who work on its privately owned cattle and sheep ranch.

Niihau is twenty-three miles long, three to six miles wide, and relatively flat. Most of its seventy square miles are under five hundred feet and its highest point, Mt. Paniau, is only 1,281 feet above sea level. While Mt. Waialeale, on Kauai, is the wettest spot in the islands, tiny Niihau gets only about twelve inches of rain a year.

Because of its size, dry climate, and lack of fresh water, Niihau has always had a small population. Today the island shelters about 250 residents. Their modest wood-frame houses, devoid of fancy plumbing and electricity, are provided by Niihau Ranch in addition to salaries, basic foods, and medical care.

The residents of Niihau are a proud people, tied to the land, and family-oriented. Hawaiian is the daily spoken language on the island and children are taught through eighth grade in Hawaiian, as well as English, in the ranch school. Students who further education are sent off-island and their tuition is paid by the ranch.

The island's pasture lands support two thousand head of cattle, three thousand wild turkeys, and twelve thousand sheep grown mostly for wool. Other exports include pond-raised mullet, honey, and charcoal made from keawe trees. Niihau is also known for the tiny seashells that residents gather off the beaches and string into beautiful leis.

Because of its small size and population, Niihau has long maintained close economic and political ties with Kauai. Neither fell into the grasp of Kamehameha I when he began to unite all of the islands under his rule in the late 1700s. It was not until 1810 that Niihau and Kauai reluctantly chose to join the kingdom.

In 1819, the year that Kamehameha I died, a young woman in Scotland, Eliza McHutcheson, married a former Royal Navy officer, Francis Sinclair. For twenty years they operated a large farm in Scotland before selling it and sailing to New Zealand in 1841.

They bought a new farm there, but tragedy struck in 1846 when Eliza lost her husband and oldest son in a shipwreck.

Left a widow with five children, Eliza managed to keep the New Zealand farm together until 1863 when she sold it for considerable profit. The family eventually settled in Honolulu, where the king offered them land stretching from the present Honolulu Hale in downtown Honolulu to Diamond Head in Waikiki. The asking price for this property, today one of the most valuable chunks of real estate in the country, was $10,000.

The Sinclairs turned down the offer because they felt the land would be unsuitable for farming. Instead they spent their $10,000 on Niihau, a deal that included an entire island as well as its native inhabitants. During the 1870s the family also bought plantation lands on the southwestern side of Kauai at Makaweli. Eliza Sinclair died there in 1892 at the age of ninety-three.

Aubrey Robinson, a grandson, became owner of Niihau after Eliza's death. When he died in 1936 the island was inherited by his children, and today it is managed by two of his own grandsons, Keith and Bruce Robinson. Like previous members of their family, they continue to protect Niihau from disruptive modern influences and, in so doing, help to perpetuate the traditional Hawaiian way of life. ■

NIIHAU VILLAGE (above): The village of Puuwai is the main settlement on Niihau. About 250 native Hawaiians live on the island. SHELL BEACH (right): Residents of Niihau regularly comb the island's beaches for the tiny shells they string into highly prized leis.

LEHUA ISLAND (above): Crescent-shaped Lehua Island is the ridge of a sunken volcanic crater off the northern tip of Niihau.

143

FATHER AND SON : A father holds his
young son during a picnic in Waimea.

Enjoying Kauai

Most visitors to Kauai, which lies sixty-five miles northwest of Oahu, arrive by plane. The main airport on Kauai is located at Lihue, a short flight from the state's international air terminal in Honolulu. It is serviced daily by Aloha Airlines, Hawaiian Airlines, and Mid Pacific Airlines. Princeville Airways has direct flights between Honolulu and Princeville, and United Airlines has nonstop flights to the island from Los Angeles.

There are several choices of transportation from the Lihue Airport to the hotel, including taxis and shuttle busses. Independent travelers will also find car rental agencies in a line of booths outside the main airport building. All of the major rental agencies and several local companies are represented. Cars are definitely a must on Kauai for self-guided tours.

From Lihue, sightseers have their pick of two main roads leading to Kauai's attractions. Highway 50 (Kaumualii Highway) runs south to Hanapepe and Waimea. Along the way, a turnoff at Highway 52 (Maluhia Road) also leads to Koloa and the Poipu resort area. Once at Waimea most visitors continue the drive up into the mountains on Highway 55 to see Waimea Canyon, Kokee State Park, and the Kalalau Valley Lookout. Highway 56 (Kuhio Highway) goes north through Wailua, Kapaa, Kilauea, and Hanalei. At the end of the road, at Haena, is Kee Beach and the beginning of the island's Na Pali Coast hiking trail.

LIHUE TO POIPU

Lihue, 103 statute miles from Honolulu, is a good starting point for island tours. The Kauai office of the Hawaii Visitors Bureau is located in the Lihue Plaza Building on Umi Street. Staff members have up-to-date information on tours, resort facilities, and scenic attractions. A large selection of brochures describing points of interest and activities is also available.

The Kauai Museum is on Rice Street. Inside are permanent exhibits on the island, its history, culture, and people. It opened in 1924 as the first public library on Kauai, and it is the finest example of the architecture that developed on the island in the 1920s.

Lihue Lutheran Church, on Hoomana Road, was built by German workers in 1883 who had come from Hanover and Bremen to work on the Lihue Plantation. The simple wooden structure, recently reconstructed, is the oldest Lutheran church in Hawaii.

Grove Farm Homestead, located off Nawiliwili Road, is a private, historical museum of plantation life on Kauai. For over a century the homestead was headquarters of Grove Farm Plantation. The original buildings and furnishings of the headquarters complex are carefully preserved today for visitors.

Nawiliwili is one mile south of Lihue. The island's main port is here, at Nawiliwili Harbor. The passenger ships *Independence* and *Constitution*, operated by American Hawaii Cruises, and the *Monterey*, operated by Aloha Pacific Cruises, call here a couple of times each week. Nearby is The Westin Kauai at Kauai Lagoons. The resort is fronted by popular Kalapaki Beach.

Huleia Stream empties into Nawiliwili Harbor, and Alekoko Fishpond, often called Menehune Fishpond, is a walled-off bend in the stream. The ancient Hawaiians, menehune or otherwise, dammed this large lagoon area to raise mullet and other food fish. An overlook provides a scenic view from Niumalu Road. Back along Highway 50, near the Nawiliwili Road intersection, is the Kukui Grove Center shopping mall.

Maluhia Road, which also turns off from Highway 50, leads through a tunnel of stately eucalyptus trees to Koloa. Here in 1835 the island's first sugar plantation, Ladd and Company (later the Koloa Plantation) was established. Surviving today are the remains of the boiling house and stone chimney of the mill which was built in 1841.

Back west along Highway 50, just beyond the Nawiliwili Road intersection, is the Kukui Grove Center shopping mall. Further on is Kilohana, the former manor home of Ethel and Gaylord Wilcox. It was built in 1935 when Wilcox was manager of Grove Farm Plantation. He named the home after Kilohana Crater, visible in the distance. The home has been restored and some of the rooms turned into small boutique shops. A restaurant named Gaylord's extends out into the courtyard.

Nearby is a circular concrete sculpture that suggests a broken granite mill stone. Inside are eight life-size bronze figures that represent the eight principal ethnic groups that helped create Kauai's prosperous sugar industry. The sculpture, by Jan Fisher, was dedicated in 1985 to mark the 150th anniversary of sugar production in the islands.

Old Koloa Town, across the street, is a planned shopping village designed around a number of quaint old renovated plantation buildings. Yamamoto Store, now occupied by a retail T-shirt shop, was constructed in 1900. Just behind is the town's oldest surviving structure, the one-story Koloa Hotel which flanks Waikomo Stream. It was built in 1898 to serve traveling salesmen who came from Honolulu to Koloa Landing by interisland steamer. Today the former hotel's five rooms house boutique shops.

Farther south is sunny Poipu, a beach resort destination containing the Waiohai Resort Hotel, Sheraton Kauai, Poipu Beach Hotel, Poipu Kai Resort, Kiahuna Plantation, and several other, smaller accommodations. Recreation facilities include the championship Kiahuna Plantation Golf Course and two dozen tennis courts. Poipu Beach Park is a favorite spot for swimming and picnics, and Spouting Horn Park is named for a geyser of water that spouts like a whale from a shoreline lava tube.

Prince Kuhio Park, in Kukuiula, commemorates the 1871 birthplace of Jonah Kuhio Kalanianaole, a royal family member who was Hawaii's delegate to the U.S. Congress from 1903 to his death in 1922. "Prince Cupid," as he was known by a childhood nickname, devoted a lifetime to public service and, in 1919, introduced the first bill proposing that Hawaii be made a state.

Forty years later, after Hawaii finally achieved that goal in 1959, Prince Kuhio's birthdate of March 26 was declared a state holiday. Each year Kauai holds a Prince Kuhio Festival in late March to honor the island's beloved native son. On a memorial plaque at Prince Kuhio Park is the Hawaiian phrase, *Ke Alii O Na Makaainana*, "The Prince of the People."

LAWAI TO KEKAHA

Lawai is the former home of Kauai Pineapple Company, founded in 1905 as the Kauai Fruit and Land Company. The cannery closed in 1964 although its buildings remain. In Lawai Valley the Pacific Tropical Botanical Garden contains 186 acres of tropical plants collected from throughout the world. Adjoining the botanical garden is the Allerton Gardens at Lawai Kai. This property originally belonged to Queen Emma, wife of Kamehameha IV. She started the gardens in the 1870s and her summer cottage still stands there.

At Kalaho a short sideroad leads to Kukuiolono Park, formerly the estate of

Walter Sinclair McBryde. From the top of the hill there is a superb view of the ocean, overlooking the island's southern coast. The park includes a small nine-hole hillside golf course. A half-mile west of Kalaheo is the Olu Pua Botanical Garden and Plantation. Once the estate garden of the Kauai Pineapple Company, it has twelve acres of landscaped grounds and theme gardens. Still present is the old plantation manager's home and other estate buildings.

From the Hanapepe Canyon Lookout the greenery of Hanapepe Valley caught between the steep red cliffs can be seen. Taro patches are present at the mouth of the canyon. In 1824 the last major battle on Kauai was fought opposite the lookout when Kaumualii led an unsuccessful revolt against troops loyal to the Kamehamehas. Over a hundred rebels were reported to have died in the battle.

The picturesque town of Hanapepe hugs the Hanapepe River. Some of the wooden buildings, in the older west bank section, hang out over the water. Farms around Hanapepe produce much of the island's produce.

Today, near Hanapepe, is found Salt Pond Beach Park, a living symbol of Kauai's rural lifestyle. Here, during the summer months, a number of local families gather rock salt from the shallow beds by using the same methods practiced by the ancient Hawaiians. The light brown salt is not sold commercially but is prized by friends of the saltmakers.

Waimea is a busy community with a prominent place in the island's history. Captain Cook landed here in 1778 and Cook Monument stands in the center of town. Kauai's oldest home is the Gulick-Rowell House on Huakai Road. This New England-style wooden structure, with its coral limestone foundation and walls, was built in 1829.

The ruins of Fort Elizabeth, often called the Russian fort, sit on the east bank of the Waimea River. It was initially constructed between 1815 and 1817 under an alliance between the Russian-American Company and King Kaumualii. The Hawaiians took over the fort in 1817 after the Russians were expelled from Kauai and occupied it until 1864 when it was dismantled.

Menehune Ditch, one-and-a-half miles down Menehune Road, is located opposite a suspension foot bridge that spans the Waimea River. This ancient waterway was once used to irrigate farm lands. Unfortunately, only a small section of the ditch, built with cut and fitted faced rock, has survived.

Highway 50 continues on past Kekaha to Mana and Barking Sands, site of the U.S. Navy Pacific Missile Range Fleet Mobile Tracking Facility. Check with the military sentry for permission to enter the area. Visitors to Polihale State Park, at the south end of Kauai's Na Pali Coast, have a good view of privately owned Niihau, fifteen miles west across the Kaulakahi Channel.

KEKAHA TO THE KALALAU VALLEY LOOKOUT

Two roads lead from Highway 55 to Waimea Canyon and Kokee State parks. Highway 55 (Kokee Road) begins in Kekaha and climbs up the mountain to the canyon and Kalalau Valley Lookout. After eight miles Highway 55 is met by the Waimea Canyon Road, which starts in Waimea and runs up along the canyon rim.

Highway 55 continues to the Waimea Canyon Lookout, three thousand feet above sea level. From here there is a grand view of the twenty-five-hundred-feet-deep gorge that is popularly called the "Grand Canyon of the Pacific." The Puu Hinahina Lookout, farther ahead, provides yet another spectacular look into the canyon.

Kokee State Park covers 4,345 acres of wilderness. The state owns the Kokee Lodge at park headquarters but it is operated by a concessionaire. Included in the operation is a restaurant, gift shop, natural history museum, and a dozen rental cabins. Visitors can also obtain maps at the lodge that outline seventeen hiking trails in the park which cover about forty-five miles.

Among the most popular are the Nature Trail, a walk of less than a mile that loops through koa tree woods to a picnic area, and the Canyon Trail, a two-mile walk that follows the north rim of Waimea Canyon and ends at Kumuwela Lookout. The longest trail takes hikers across the damp and muddy Alakai Swamp.

The road past Kokee Lodge climbs up still farther to the Kalalau Lookout. From this four-thousand-foot-high observation point there is a panoramic, though often cloud-covered, view of Kalalau Valley extending all the way to the sea. Hiking is not permitted into the valley from the lookout.

LIHUE TO ANAHOLA

The 10-mile stretch from Lihue to Kapaa is called the "Coconut Coast" by the area's marketing association. It got its nickname from the many coconut trees which grow along the eastern shore of the Garden Island.

North out of Lihue the highway meets Maalo Road at Kapaia. This narrow sideroad leads four miles to Wailua Falls.

Continuing on Highway 56 the plantation village of Hanamaulu includes shops in several wooden false-front buildings. The Kauai Hilton and Beach Villas are located along a stretch of Hanamaulu Beach.

The Hanamaulu-Ahukini cutoff road links Kuhio Highway north of Hanamaulu with Kapule Highway at Ahukini Road in Lihue. Visitors will find that the road allows easy access to Lihue Airport.

Further ahead, on the ocean side of the highway, is Lydgate State Park. This is the site of an ancient temple of refuge which provided sanctuary to Hawaiians in time of trouble. Today there are picnic facilities and campgrounds at the park.

Wailua Marina is located at the mouth of the Wailua River, the largest and only navigable river in the state. The marina is the staging area for frequent daily trips to the Fern Grotto by both Smith's Motor Boat Service and Waialeale Boat Tours. A popular site for island weddings, the Fern Grotto is a large but shallow lava tube cave that is naturally trimmed with thousands of ferns.

At the mouth of the river, opposite the marina, is Coco Palms, the island's oldest major hotel. This site and its century-old lagoon was once the home of Deborah Kapule. The fifteen-hundred-tree coconut grove that gives the hotel its name was originally planted in 1896.

Highway 58, which turns up into the mountains past Coco Palms, is sometimes called the King's Highway because of its use by the early Hawaiian monarchs. Just past the coconut grove is Holo-Holo-Ku. This temple site, the oldest found to date on the island, was one of the few places in ancient Hawaii where human sacrifices were offered to the gods. At the southwest corner of the ruins is a large rock upon which the victims were killed.

Nearby is Pohaku-Ho-o Hanau, a group of sacred stones where the women of royalty came to give birth. The sanded platform in front of the stones was once the floor of a shelter erected to protect the expectant mothers. Beyond these birth-stones, at the top of the hill, was once located the king's house and private temple. Another trail below leads to a Bell Stone that was rung to announce, among other things, the birth of the royal infants.

Farther ahead visitors can look down to the bank of the Wailua River and the grass houses that comprise Kamokila Hawaiian Village, a replica of an ancient Kauai fishing community. Visitors to the site are entertained by music, dance, games, and demonstrations of traditional Hawaiian arts and crafts. Nearby is also a view of Opaekaa Falls, a name which means "rolling shrimp." Shrimp tumble around in the water at the foot of the falls while laying their eggs.

Back on Highway 56, between Wailua and Kapaa, is the Coconut Plantation, an eighty-acre hotel and condominium development at Waipouli. The complex includes the Sheraton Coconut Beach Hotel, the Kauai Beach Boy Hotel, the Islander on the Beach, and other accommodations. Here, too, is The Market Place at Coconut Plantation, a popular shopping center of over seventy stores and snack shops.

Kapaa, the island's second largest town, is a revitalized plantation town where modern architecture sits alongside revitalized old buildings. Among the most interesting historic structures are the Seto Building, Hee Fat Building, and the Awapuhi Store. All Saints Church, erected in 1925, was the first Episcopal Church building on Kauai.

Highway 56 continues through the scenic seaside. The turnoff at Kealia Road goes up to St. Catherine's Catholic Church. It is a modern building that's noted for its religious paintings and ceramic work by Jean Charlot, Juliette May Fraser, and Tseng Yu-ho. Anahola Beach Park, on Anahola Bay, has good picnic facilities. It is often uncrowded because of its remote location.

KILAUEA TO HAENA

Kilauea's beginnings can be traced to the 1870s and the establishment of the Kilauea Sugar Plantation. The company is gone now, but the community that remains is close-knit and tied to its past by a relatively large number of stone buildings around town. Leading this architectural list is the large plantation manager's house, constructed in 1928.

The most unusual store in Kilauea is the Kong Lung Company, located in a stone building constructed in 1941. Formerly a Chinese plantation store (the business actually dates back to 1881), Kong Lung's present owners carry an inventory of fine quality housewares and Oriental merchandise.

Another recommended stop in Kilauea is at St. Sylvester Catholic Church. This octagonal stone structure is a church-in-the-round with pews that nearly encircle the altar. The paintings of the stations of the cross are also by Jean Charlot. Also noted for its interesting architecture is Christ Memorial Church. It contains a hand carved altar and stained glass windows made in England.

Kilauea Lighthouse is located outside of town, on the tip of a peninsula about two hundred feet above the sea. This is the northernmost point of the inhabited Hawaiian Islands. Built in 1913, the inactive lighthouse is fifty-two feet high and once guided ships from the Orient past Kauai and on to Oahu. Its clamshell lens is the largest of its type ever made. Now the lighthouse stands guard over a wildlife sanctuary noted for its seabirds. The interior of the lighthouse is closed to the public but there is a visitors center, gift shop, and public restrooms in the small park.

Princeville Airport is the air link to this side of the island. In addition to commuter planes, the airport services sightseeing helicopters which provide dramatic tours above the island.

Several miles farther on is Princeville at Hanalei, a planned resort community that includes single family homes, townhouses, the Princeville Shopping Center, Sheraton Princeville Hotel, and a dramatically designed twenty-seven-hole championship golf course.

The prestigious development took its name from Princeville Ranch, the oldest ranch on Kauai. It was founded in 1853 by Robert Crichton Wyllie, a Scotsman, who served the Hawaiian Kingdom as minister of foreign affairs. He called the ranch Princeville following a two-week visit of Kamehameha IV, Queen Emma, and their two-year-old son, Prince Albert. Sadly, the young prince died two years later.

Just past Princeville is the Hanalei Valley Lookout, which presents one of the most photographed views in the islands. Hanalei River runs through the center of the valley's taro farms on its way to the ocean.

In the middle of the valley, close to the river, is the historic Haraguchi Rice Mill. The last of its kind in the islands, the mill was operated by the Haraguchi family from 1924 until it ceased operations in 1960. Now restored, it spotlights the story of the valley's rice industry.

The road descends after the lookout and crosses the old narrow steel bridge which was erected in 1912. Hanalei is a fairly quiet beach town today, but when rice production was at its peak in the 1930s this was a busy island port. The bay, with its concrete pier, is popular with swimmers and surfers but its big waves and strong currents are dangerous during the winter months.

In 1834 the Protestant missionaries started a mission on the banks of the Waioli River; the Waioli Mission House, now operated as a museum, was built in 1837. The Waioli Mission Hall, originally the church, opened its doors in 1841 and the roadside Waioli Huiia Church, with its high

peaked roof and belfry, was added to the mission grounds in 1912.

There are a number of excellent beaches between Hanalei and Haena, including Lumahai Beach which was used in the movie *South Pacific*. A steep trail leads down to this beach but swimming is not recommended. Across the road from Haena County Park is the Maniniholo Dry Cave, named after the head fisherman of the menehune. It is actually the mouth of a lava tube that runs under the cliff. Farther ahead are the wet caves of Waikapalae and Waikanaloa that local folklore says were dug by the goddess Pele.

Wainiha is a small community of mostly local Hawaiian families. The perpetual waterfalls in the Wainiha Valley generate electrical power for half the island with power lines crossing the mountains from the north shore to Waimea and Hanapepe.

Highway 56 ends in Haena at Kee Beach. A path from the quiet cove leads up along the shoreline to the remains of an ancient hula heiau linked to the Pele, Hiiaka, and Lohiau legends. The eleven-mile trail along Na Pali Coast to Kalalau Valley also begins near the beach.

MUSEUMS

GROVE FARM HOMESTEAD
P.O. Box 1631
Lihue, Kauai, HI 96766
Tel. 808-245-3202

Guided tours of this former sugar plantation headquarters are given every Monday, Wednesday, and Thursday. Tour times are 10 a.m. and 1:15 p.m. and last about two hours. Make reservations in advance. Admission charge.

KAUAI MUSEUM
4428 Rice St.
Lihue, Kauai, HI 96766
Tel. 808-245-6931

A two-building complex containing historical, cultural, and artistic exhibits. A gift shop specializes in books about Hawaii, maps, and prints. Open Monday through Friday from 9:30 a.m. to 4:30 p.m. Admission charge.

KILAUEA LIGHTHOUSE
P.O. Box 87
Kilauea, Kauai, HI 96752
Tel. 808-828-1431

The gift shop and bird sanctuary grounds surrounding the lighthouse are open Sunday through Friday from 12 noon to 4 p.m. No admission charge.

KOKEE NATURAL HISTORY MUSEUM
Kokee State Park
P.O. Box 518
Kekaha, Kauai, HI 96752
Tel. 808-335-9974
Open daily. No admission charge.

KAMOKILA VILLAGE
6060 Kuamoo Road
Kapaa, Kauai, HI 96746
Tel: 808-822-1192

This replica of an ancient Hawaiian village (on an authentic site) is located on the banks of the Waialua River. Inside this "living museum," local islanders give demonstrations of traditional Hawaiian arts, crafts, sports, the hula, and food preparation. Open Monday through Saturday from 9:30 a.m. to 4 p.m. Admission charge.

KILOHANA
P.O. Box 3121
Lihue, Kauai, HI 96766
Tel: 808-245-5608

This English Tudor manor was originally built as a plantation home in 1935. It has now been restored with period furniture, antiques, and artwork to reflect the best of island living in the 1930s. Retail shops and restaurants are located inside the house and in former guest cottages on the 35-acre estate. No admission charge. Shops open daily from 9 a.m. to 7:30 p.m. Restaurants open to 10 p.m.

WAIOLI MISSION HOUSE
Hanalei, Kauai, HI 96766
Tel. 808-245-3202

Guided tours of this 1837 missionary home are given Tuesday through Saturday from 9 a.m. to 12 p.m. and 1 p.m. to 3 p.m. No reservations required. No admission charge but donations are accepted.

GARDENS

KIAHUNA GARDENS
Poipu Beach, Kauai, HI 96756
Tel. 808-742-6411

Self-guided tours on marked trails. Open daily from 9 a.m. to 6 p.m. No admission charge.

OLU PUA BOTANICAL GARDEN AND PLANTATION
P.O. Box 518
Kalaheo, Kauai, HI 96741
Tel. 808-332-8182

Botanical garden on a twelve-acre plantation manager's estate. Open 8:30 a.m. to 5 p.m. daily. Guided tours on Monday, Wednesday, and Friday at 1:15 p.m. and 3:15 p.m. Admission charge.

PACIFIC TROPICAL BOTANICAL GARDEN
P.O. Box 340
Lawai, Kauai, HI 96765
Tel. 808-332-8131

The only national, privately supported tropical botanical garden chartered by U.S. Congress. Office hours Monday through Friday from 7:30 a.m. to 4 p.m. Call for tour information. Admission charge.

SMITH'S TROPICAL PARADISE
R.R. 1, Box 252-P
Kapaa, Kauai, HI 96746
Tel. 808-822-4654

Botanical garden located on thirty acres near the Wailua Marina. Open Monday through Friday from 10 a.m. to 5 p.m. Admission charge.

NIIHAU TOURS

Aerial sightseeing tours to Niihau are now permitted by the private owners of the island. These unique tours are conducted exclusively by Niihau Helicopters with a twin-engine helicopter that is also used by Niihau's residents for medical emergency flights. The Niihau tour includes one landing near the shoreline. Niihau Helicopters (808-335-3500) is located just west of Hanapepe in Kaumakani. Hours are 8 a.m. to 5 p.m. Monday through Friday.

WAILUA RIVER BOAT TOURS

Boat trips up the Wailua River to the Fern Grotto are among the most popular tours on Kauai. Two companies, Smith's Motor Boat Service (808-822-5213) and Waialeale Boat Tours (808-822-4908) operate out of Wailua Marina near the mouth of the river. Hawaiian music and hula is presented aboard the boats which leave about every half-hour between 9 a.m. and 4 p.m. There are also night dinner cruises several times a week which feature a candlelit visit to the Fern Grotto.

WATER ACTIVITIES

It would be hard to find a more perfect place than Kauai for water-related activities. Beachcombers have their favorite spots and there are good swimming areas all around the island. Among the other popular watersports on Kauai are snorkeling, scuba diving, surfing, windsurfing, waterskiing, Zodiac rafting, kayaking, wave skiing, and small craft sailing. Check with the hotel travel desk and tourist publications for companies renting equipment.

FISHING AND HUNTING

Kauai offers every kind of fishing, from freshwater flycasting in Kokee's mountain streams to polefishing off the Hanalei Pier. Spearfishing and surfcasting are also popular. Charter boats can be rented for deep sea fishing after marlin, wahoo, bonito, ono, and yellow-fin tuna.

Each year the state stocks Kokee's mountain streams with fingerling rainbow trout to support a fishing season that usually starts in early August and runs through the end of September. The fish do not reproduce in the streams because, even this high up, the water does not get cold enough.

Hunters go after wild boar, feral goats, blacktail deer, and numerous game birds. Licenses are required. For information contact the State Division of Fish and Game, Department of Land and Natural Resources, Lihue, Kauai, HI 96766; 808-245-4444.

HORSEBACK RIDING

Horses have long been the favored means of travel in Kauai's ranch country. Youngsters are taught to groom and ride early in life, and the fit of a saddle is second nature by the time they reach their teens. Highgate Ranch (808-822-3182) in Wailua Homestead, CMJ Country Stables (808-245-6666) in Koloa, and Pooku Stables (808-826-6777) in Hanalei all provide riding horses by the hour or day. Longer camping trips can also be arranged. Western and English saddles are available.

GOLF AND TENNIS

Kauai has several excellent golf courses, all open to the public. The most celebrated is the Princeville Makai Golf Course (808-826-3580) at Princeville. It was designed by Robert Trent Jones, Jr. Other courses are the Kiahuna Plantation Golf Course (808-742-9595) in Poipu, the Kukuiolono Golf Course (808-332-9151) in Kalaheo, the Wailua Municipal Golf Course (808-332-9151), and the Kauai Lagoons and Kiele Lagoons golf courses—both designed by Jack Nicklaus—at The Westin Kauai (808-245-5050). All of the major hotels have tennis courts for their guests and a few make their courts available to nonguests. Free public tennis courts can be used in Lihue, Kalaheo, Hanapepe, Waimea, and Kapaa.

HIKING AND CAMPING

Kauai, with its extensive wilderness areas, is an ideal island for hiking and camping. There are miles of trails in Kokee State Park and the island's Na Pali Coast is the best-known hiking area in Hawaii. No permit is needed. Camping, which does require a permit, is allowed in numerous places on the island.

For information and permits for county parks contact the Division of Parks and Recreation, County of Kauai, 4191 Hardy St., Lihue, Kauai, HI 96766; 808-245-4982. For state parks contact the Division of State Parks, Department of Land and Natural Resources, 3060 Eiwa St., Lihue, Kauai, HI 96766; 808-245-4444.

Several local companies and organizations provide guided hiking and camping trips. These include Hanalei Camping and Backpacking, Kauai Scenic Hikes, Kauai Sports, Sierra Club, Local Boy Tours, YMCA, and YWCA.

The only state-owned cabins for rent in the entire state are located at Kokee Lodge. Units vary in size from one large room, which sleeps three, to two-bedroom cabins that can accommodate seven. All twelve of the current cabins are furnished with refrigerators, stoves, hot showers, basic eating and cooking utensils, linens, towels, blankets, and pillows. Each cabin has a fireplace and chopped wood is available.

According to park rules the Kokee cabins can be rented for a maximum length of five days. Pets are not permitted. Reservations should be made months in advance. For information contact the Kokee Lodge, P. O. Box 819, Waimea, Kauai, HI 96796; 808-335-6061.

PERIODICALS

Two main newspapers serve Kauai. *The Garden Island*, published four times a week, got its start in 1902. The more recent *Kauai Times* is published weekly. Local news is also available from the *Honolulu Advertiser* which publishes a neighbor island edition each morning.

Visitors may pick up several complimentary publications for road maps, tips on island touring, and shopping suggestions. These include the *Kauai Drive Guide* (which is given out with rental cars), the *Kauai Beach Press*, *Spotlight Kauai*, and *This Week Kauai*. Sturdivant Publishing has publications for particular areas of Kauai—*Poipu Beach Guide*, *Coconut Coast Guide*, *Princeville/Hanalei Guide*, as well as golf guides for the major resorts.

HAWAIIAN WORDS

Hawaiian remained a spoken language until 1829 when the Calvinist-Christian missionaries selected a 12-letter alphabet. They voted to establish the consonants as h, k, l, m, n, p and w. Vowel sounds are a, e, i, o, u. All words in the Hawaiian language end in a vowel and consonants do not occur without vowels between them. Words do not change to indicate tenses and there are no endings to indicate the plural. Today an okina (') is used to mark the glottal stop of written Hawaiian words and a macron, or line above a vowel (e.g., a), is used to indicate long vowel sounds. Except for the word Kaua'i, as used in the title of this book, all other Hawaiian words within the text are printed without the okina or macron.

Hawaii Visitors Bureau
Island of Kauai
3016 Umi Street
Suite 207
Lihue, Kauai, HI 96766
Tel. (808) 245-3971

Daily Weather Information
Tel. (808) 245-6001

Marine Forecast
Tel. (808)245-3564

Selected Readings

Aikin, Ross R. *Kilauea Point Lighthouse.* Kilauea: Kilauea Point Natural History Association, 1988.

Barriere, Dorothy B., Mary Kawena Pukui, and Marion Kelly. *Hula: Historical Perspectives.* Honolulu: Bishop Museum Press, 1980.

Barrow, Terence. *Captain Cook in Hawaii.* Honolulu: Island Heritage, 1976.

Beaglehole, J. C. *The Life of Captain James Cook.* Stanford: Stanford University Press, 1974.

Bennett, Wendall C. *Archaeology of Kauai.* Honolulu: Bernice P. Bishop Museum Bulletin 80, 1931.

Brennan, Joseph. *Paniolo.* Honolulu: Topgallant Publishing Company, 1978.

Chisholm, Craig. *Hawaiian Hiking Trails.* (Rev. ed.) Lake Oswego, Oregon: The Fernglen Press: 1985.

Daws, Gavan. *Shoal of Time: A History of the Hawaiian Islands.* New York: The Macmillan Co., 1968. Reprint 1974. Honolulu: University of Hawaii Press.

Day, A. Grove. (ed.) *Stories of Hawaii by Jack London.* New York: Appleton-Century, 1965. Reprint 1984. Honolulu: Mutual Publishing Company.

Donohugh, Don, and Bea Donohugh. *Kauai: A Paradise Guide.* Portland: Paradise Publications, 1988.

Duffy, Warren. *Kauai's Incredible North Shore.* Hanalei: Island Enterprises Books, 1983.

Gay, Lawrence K. *Tales of the Forbidden Island of Niihau.* Honolulu: Topgallant Publishing Co. Ltd., 1981.

Gurnani-Smith, Ruth. *The Essential Guide to Kauai.* Honolulu: Island Heritage, 1988.

Hind, Norman E. A. *The Geology of Kauai and Niihau.* Honolulu: Bernice P. Bishop Museum Bulletin 71, 1930.

Hopkins, Jerry. *The Hula.* Hong Kong: Apa Productions, 1982.

Hoverson, Martha, ed. *Historic Koloa: A Guide.* Friends of the Koloa Community/School Library, 1985.

Joesting, Edward. *Hawaii: An Uncommon History.* New York: W. W. Norton & Co., 1972.

Joesting, Edward. *Kauai: The Separate Kingdom.* Honolulu: University of Hawaii Press, 1984.

Kelly, Marion. *Pele and Hi'iaka Visit the Sites at Ke'e, Ha'ena, Island of Kaua'i.* Honolulu: Bishop Museum Press, 1984.

Krauss, Bob. *Kauai.* Honolulu: Island Heritage, 1978.

Krauss, Bob, and William P. Alexander. *Grove Farm Plantation.* Palo Alto: Pacific Books, 1965.

London, Jack. *The House of Pride.* New York: Macmillan, 1912.

Moriarty, Linda Paik. *Niihau Shell Leis.* Honolulu: University of Hawaii Press, 1986.

Peebles, Douglas, and Jeri Bostwick. *Pua Nani: Hawaii is a Garden.* Honolulu: Mutual Publishing, 1987.

Rice, William Hyde. *Hawaiian Legends.* Honolulu: Bishop Museum Press, New Edition, 1977.

Ronck, Ronn. *Ronck's Hawaii Almanac.* Honolulu: University of Hawaii Press, 1984.

Schleck, Robert J. *The Wilcox Quilts in Hawaii.* Lihue: Grove Farm Homestead & Waioli Mission House, 1987.

Smith, Robert. *Hiking Kauai.* Berkeley: Wilderness Press, 1977.

Stearns, Harold T. *Geology of the State of Hawaii.* Palo Alto: Pacific Books, 1985.

Valier, Kathy. *On the Na Pali Coast.* Honolulu: University of Hawaii Press, 1988.

Von Holt, Ida Elizabeth Knudsen. *Stories of Long Ago: Niihau, Kauai, Oahu.* Honolulu: Daughters of Hawaii (Rev. Ed.), 1985.

Wenkam, Robert. *Kauai: Hawaii's Garden Island.* Chicago: Rand McNally & Company, 1979.

Wichman, Frederick B. *Kauai Tales.* Honolulu, Bamboo Ridge Press, 1985.

Wilcox, Carol. *The Kauai Album.* Lihue: Kauai Historical Society, 1981.

About the Photography

O f all the Hawaiian Islands, I have visited Kauai most often. The photographs in this book were taken over a ten-year period. The first trip I took on Kauai was along the Kalalau Trail on the island's Na Pali Coast. It is only eleven miles long but, with a heavy backpack, it is a torturous two-day hike, up and down the cliffs and with innumerable switchbacks.

During the second day I kept thinking that the valley would be just around the next ridge (I had such thoughts about twenty-five times before I was finally right) and in a couple of places the trail was so narrow and the cliffs so steep that I practically had to hang on by my fingernails. But I loved it and have been back many times, though now I usually go in by kayak.

Technically, the majority of photographs in this book were taken with 35mm Nikon cameras. My film was mostly Kodachrome 64 although I have also started shooting some Fujichrome 50, with excellent results. This book also includes a few panoramas done with a Widelux.

I have used just about every camera Nikon makes and Nikkor lenses from 16mm to 500mm. Since I do not keep records while I am in the field it is difficult to say what camera or lens I used for every photo. If I am staying close to the car or in a helicopter, however, I usually take a large camera bag with two bodies and the following lenses: 16mm, 20mm, 28mm, 35mm, 105mm, and a 80–200 zoom for telephoto. On long hikes I will just take one camera with a 28mm, a 105mm, and a light tripod.

This is the type of shooting I especially enjoy in Kauai with its shades of green, deep blue ocean, and incredible beaches. Kauai is special to me, and I always look for any excuse to go back.

Douglas Peebles

Index

155

Special thanks from Douglas Peebles to Margaret; from Ronn Ronck to Amelia and Cindy. Also to Galyn Wong, Edward Joesting, Tony Kunimura, David Penhallow, Maile Asing Semitekol, Sheila Donnelly, Doreen Leland, Lopaka Mansfield, Jimmy and Joyce Miranda, Patty Ewing, Red Johnson, Papillon Helicopters, Lana Rosa, Michael Faye, Darryl and Jane Kaneshiro, Arthur and Lena Palama, Ernest Sueoka, Guy Buffet, Mrs. Charles A. Rice, Val Knudsen, Rerioterai Tava, Paul Weissich, Stanley Hong, Marcie Carroll, and Jan TenBruggencate.

Photographed by Douglas Peebles
Written by Ronn Ronck
Produced by Bennett Hymer

Art direction: Bill Fong
Design: Leo Gonzalez and Peter Matsukawa
Design Assistants: Lisa Lindbo and
    Debra Michimoto
Editorial Assistant: Lori Ackerman

Headline type: Helvetica Black/italic
Text type: Goudy Old Style
Captions: Goudy Old Style Italic
Vignette text: Goudy Old Style italic
Typesetting by Innovative Media, Inc.
    and Ad Type

Mutual Publishing of Honolulu

Printed and bound in Singapore by
Toppan Printing Co. (S) Pte. Ltd.

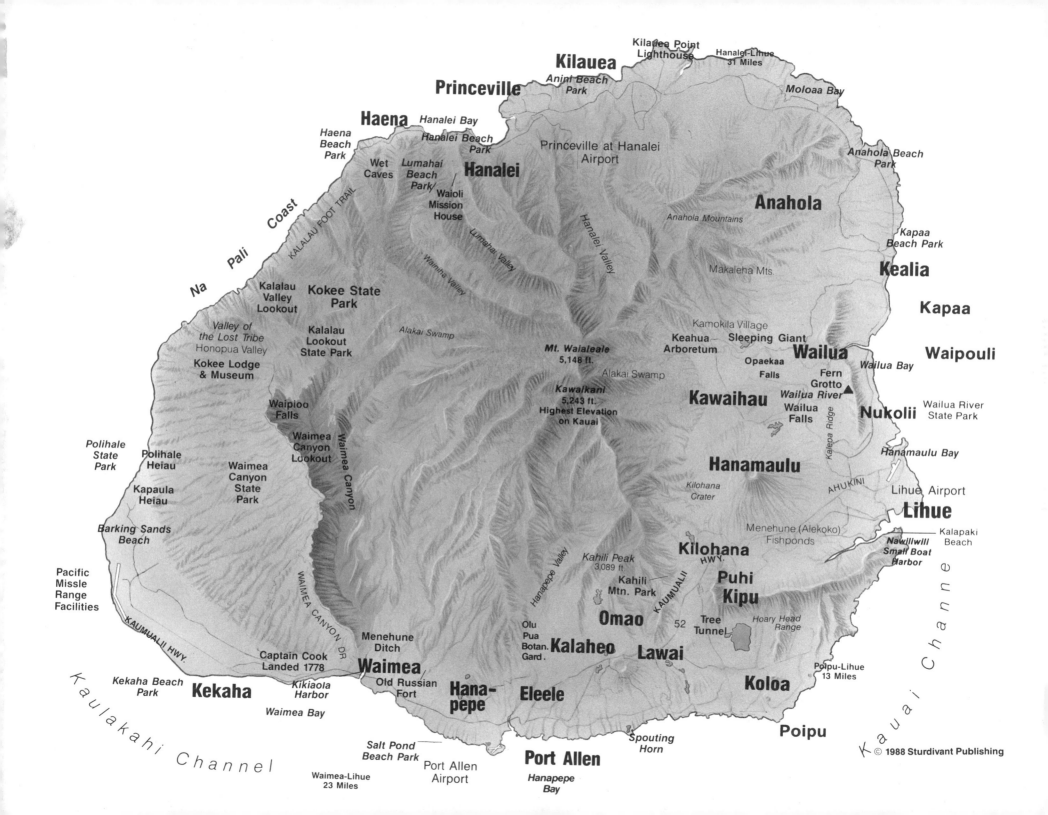

Kilauea Point
Lighthouse

Hanalei-Lihue
31 Miles

Kilauea

*Anini Beach
Park*

Moloaa Bay

Princeville

Hanalei Bay

Haena

*Haena
Beach
Park*

*Hanalei Beach
Park*

Princeville at Hanalei
Airport

*Anahola Beach
Park*

Wet
Caves

*Lumahai
Beach
Park*

Hanalei

*Waioli
Mission
House*

Anahola

*Kapaa
Beach Park*

Anahola Mountains

Na

Lumahai Valley

Hanalei Valley

Pali

KALALAU FOOT TRAIL

Wainiha Valley

Kealia

Coast

Kalalau
Valley
Lookout

**Kokee State
Park**

Makaleha Mts.

Kapaa

Alakai Swamp

Kamokila Village

Keahua
Arboretum

Sleeping Giant

Waipouli

Kalalau
Lookout
State Park

*Valley of
the Lost Tribe*
Honopua Valley

Mt. Waialeale
5,148 ft.

Alakai Swamp

Opaekaa
Falls

Wailua

Wailua Bay

Kokee Lodge
& Museum

*Fern
Grotto*

Wailua River

*Wailua River
State Park*

Kawaihau

Waipioo
Falls

Kawaikani
5,243 ft.
Highest Elevation
on Kauai

Wailua
Falls

Nukolii

*Polihale
State
Park*

Polihale
Heiau

Waimea
Canyon
Lookout

Waimea Canyon

Hanamaulu

Kalepa Ridge

Hanamaulu Bay

Kapaula
Heiau

**Waimea
Canyon
State
Park**

*Kilohana
Crater*

AHUKINI

Lihue Airport

Menehune (Alekoko)
Fishponds

Lihue

*Barking Sands
Beach*

Kilohana
HWY.

*Kalapaki
Beach*

Kahili Peak
3,089 ft.

Hanapepe Valley

Kahili
Mtn. Park

**Puhi
Kipu**

*Nawiliwili
Small Boat
Harbor*

**Pacific
Missle
Range
Facilities**

WAIMEA CANYON DR.

Olu
Pua
Botan.
Gard.

Omao

52

KAUMUALII

Tree
Tunnel

*Hoary Head
Range*

KAUMUALII HWY.

Menehune
Ditch

Kalaheo

Lawai

Poipu-Lihue
13 Miles

*Kekaha Beach
Park*

Captain Cook
Landed 1778

Waimea

Old Russian
Fort

Koloa

Kekaha

Kikiaola
Harbor

**Hana-
pepe**

Eleele

Waimea Bay

*Spouting
Horn*

Poipu

*Salt Pond
Beach Park*

Port Allen
Airport

Port Allen

© 1988 Sturdivant Publishing

Kaulakahi Channel

Waimea-Lihue
23 Miles

*Hanapepe
Bay*

Kauai Channel